ADAM T

PRESENTS

VOLUME 2

BUSINESS LEADERS
EDITION

MONEY MATTERS

World's Leading Entrepreneurs Reveal their TOP TIPS TO SUCCESS

ADAM TORRES AND
ANGY CHIN

Century City, CA

ENTER TO

WIN PRIZES

from *Money Matters* Top Tips

Scan the QR Code for entry into the contest.

SCAN ME

WIN HERE

Follow Money Matters Top Tips to learn from the stories of other entrepreneurs, executives, and business owners.

Subscribe to the blog: **www.MoneyMattersTopTips.com**
Podcast: **www.MoneyMattersTopTips.com/Podcast**
Facebook: **www.facebook.com/AskAdamTorres**
Instagram: **www.instagram.com/AskAdamTorres**
Twitter: **www.twitter.com/AskAdamTorres**

Contest subject to terms and conditions listed on website.
No purchase necessary to participate.

For information, visit **www.MrCenturyCity.com**

Edited by:
Adam Torres, Claire Skinner

Managing Editor:
Melea Bullock

Graphic Design:
Kendra Cagle

MONEY
MATTERS

Century City, CA 90067
www.MrCenturyCity.com

ISBN 13: 978-1-949680-21-8

Money Matters, Beverly Hills, CA

This publication is intended to provide general information regarding the subject matter covered. However, laws and practices often vary from state to state and are subject to change. Because each factual situation is different, specific advice should be customized to the particular circumstances. For this reason, the reader is advised to consult with his or her own adviser regarding that individual's specific scenario.

This book was created as a collaborative effort. Each author's opinion is solely their own. The authors have taken reasonable precautions in the preparation of this book and think the facts shown in the book are accurate as of the date it was written. However, neither the authors nor the publisher assume any responsibility for any liability resulting from the use or application of the information contained in this book, and the information is not intended to serve as legal or professional advice related to individual situations.

DEDICATION

To God who gave me this opportunity to share.

To my husband & best friend Amos Chin who has always supported me throughout my entrepreneurial journey.

You are the fire that keeps my entrepreneurial spirit burning. Thank you for everything.

TABLE OF CONTENTS

ACKNOWLEDGEMENTS

Special thanks to my family and friends who believed in me when I started BIC Group and who have always supported my entrepreneurial journey:

1. Mike Abadi, CEO, California Solar Exchange
2. Eddie Abraamyan, CEO, EZ Inflatables
3. Patricia Almeida, COO, The LIV Group
4. Michael Arayata, VP of Finance, Bryant Rubber
5. Jon Arima, CEO, Arima Business Solutions
6. Brogan Bryant, CEO, Bryant Rubber
7. Steven Bryant, Chairman, Bryant Rubber
8. Napoleon Canizales, CEO, Givit
9. Nancy Caron
10. Jenny Chen, Manager, J&S Beauty
11. Toshimi Chida
12. Amos Chin
13. Ryan Choura, CEO, Choura Events
14. Kien Tong, Kim, Marcus, and Nicky Chua
15. Brandin Cohen, CEO, The LIV Group
16. Michael Cole, Partner, Holthouse, Carlin & Van Trigt
17. Danny and Tracey Daniel, Founders, Trans International Trucking
18. Emily Diaz
19. Melinda Diaz, Controller, Overland, Pacific & Cutler
20. Allan P. Donnelly, Attorney, Law Offices of Allan P. Donnelly
21. Brian Everett, CEO, Overland, Pacific & Cutler
22. Tzvi Ferszt, President, TDI Properties
23. Tessie Gaa, Manager, R&D Incentives Group
24. Quan Gan, CEO, ZTag.com

25. Asghar Ghassemy, CEO, UniVoIP
26. Tami Graham
27. Jason Higa, CEO, Zippy's Restaurants
28. Daniel Hsieh, US Bank
29. Debbie Hu, General Manager, KWA Performance Industries
30. Mae Ling Hum, Manager, AT&T
31. Robert Kaminski, CEO, Impetus Leadership Advisory Group
32. Karen Kashanian, Operations Manager, TDI Properties
33. Jeff Kausek, CEO, DeFi Technologies
34. Alexa Kayekjian, Commercial Banker, First Foundation Bank
35. Shannon Kelly, President, Choura Events
36. Jason Kim, CEO, Hapa Foods
37. Nora Lau, CAO, B2Sign
38. Paul Liu, CEO, B2Sign
39. Miriam Macias, CEO, Alerce Reporting
40. Marat Manucharyan, SVP, City National Bank
41. Kevin Martin, COO, Twenty Four 7 Global Solutions
42. Laura Martinez
43. Daren Mesrobian, Principal, Holthouse, Carlin & Van Trigt
44. Sal Mixquitl
45. Sam Newman, CEO, YSN Imports
46. Michael Patrick, Client Executive, Marsh & McLennan Agency
47. Nick Payab, COO, UniVoIP
48. Dana Ramirez
49. Logan Ross
50. Susan Ruth, Director, The Aerospace Corporation
51. Dr. Meredith Sagan
52. Raz Savad
53. Laura Schneider, Partner, CPA Collective

54. Robin Schneider, CEO, Llumetec
55. Israel Schochet, President, YSN Imports
56. LiJun Sun, CEO, HealthAll Consulting
57. Mihoko Tanabe, Program Director, Long Beach Japanese Language School
58. Joe Wachtel, CEO, Monkey Wrench Plumbing
59. Phillip Walker, CEO, Network Solutions Provider
60. Yen Weng, VP, City National Bank
61. Karen Wong
62. Barry Woon, CEO, Twenty Four 7 Global Solutions
63. Alice Yang, Virtualization System Administrator/Information Assurance Analyst, Northrop Grumman
64. James, Lisa, Jason Yeh, Owners, Value Wholesaler
65. Ivan Yeo, Software Development Engineer, Amazon
66. Susie Yu, Owner, J&S Beauty
67. Dean and Jane Lee
68. Sally Lee
69. Drew Goodwin
70. Inori Fukuda

FOREWORD

By **ADAM TORRES**

Every day, I interview business leaders on the Money Matters Top Tips podcast. What started as an experiment to promote books sales by providing rich content people could use has turned into a bit of an obsession. On Friday afternoon when it's time to stop recording, I'm already looking at the calendar for who I have lined up to interview next week. When Sunday morning comes around I feel the adrenaline starting to pump getting ready for Monday mornings' recording session. And Sunday night, well, I feel like a kid getting ready for their first day of school. I'm anxious to go to sleep and wake up already to the new day's possibilities.

Why all the fuss? Let me explain. My entire life I've been a reader. A person who constantly seeks knowledge. For much of my life, I wouldn't even allow a television in my home, but I always had stocked bookshelves brimming with new treats. My taste varies but one of my favorite things to read are biographies. To me, reading biographies is one of the best ways to piece together the lives of those who have paved the way before us. To harness their knowledge and lessons from the good and bad which took place in their lives. I didn't know it then, but I always wanted to get closer to the source of knowledge, the actual person.

While I can't get Abraham Lincoln on my podcast for obvious reasons, I can connect directly with the people who are making history now. It serves as an outlet to help those who seek knowledge and guidance, and it can even give someone a sense of feeling connected through shared experience. For example, sometimes a guest will mention how a business they started failed miserably. As they go through the details of why it failed, I sit quietly while cringing, thinking, "Been there, done that."

I'm sure some of the people driving in their cars or sitting in their offices are also wincing when they listen to the episode, remembering their own failed endeavors. I also like to think that just maybe there is a young, less experienced entrepreneur listening to that same episode taking notes and possibly avoiding some of the pitfalls of inexperience by learning from the lessons of the seasoned business leader being interviewed. The goal is for the Money Matters Top Tips podcast to save people time and money while inspiring action motivated by purpose.

Following are just a few bits of sage advice guests have shared on the podcast. Whenever one of these one liners move me, I can't help but get it up on twitter @AskAdamTorres.

"Always ask yourself, does your product serve a need, greed, or vanity?"

"Don't disrupt what people are talking about, become what they are talking about."

"If you can get comfortable approaching people you don't know, you can get really comfortable approaching people you do know."

"Get to know people who can write big checks."

"Operate in reality when running your business."

"Money matters but mission matters, too."

"If you do nothing, nothing happens. If you enter the door, there is always an exit."

Now that you know a little more about why I do what I do, let's talk more about why the book you are holding in your hands was created.

I believe that platforms such as podcasts and books should be used to get the best information out to the most amount of people possible. Ideally, knowledge from the people who are making history today. I've found that getting information like this is often difficult. Why? Well, because unless they are in the business of publishing, it's not likely business leaders like these have time to sit down and write a book! They are busy running their businesses and making a difference.

Given the complexity of putting together a project like this, it is with great pride that I present to you a book of today's leaders who have sacrificed their time coming together in this collaborative work to give you their best for the greater good. In this book, you will find 18 chapters each written by a different business leader and packed full of lessons, tips, and words of wisdom. Topics range from "Empowerment to Drive Accountability" to "Technology Private Equity Done Right" and many more. The book is not written in chronological order, so feel free to skip around and explore. Consider this your business leadership playground and enjoy!

To share your stories, connect with me on Instagram:
@AskAdamTorres

Wishing you much success,

Adam Torres

INTRODUCTION

By **ANGY CHIN**

Congrats on being an entrepreneur, or perhaps you are thinking about being one soon. Let's get the bad news out of the way.

Most small businesses fail. According to Small Business Association (SBA) and Bureau of Labor Statistics, half of all small businesses will not make it past their 5th year. Success rate is very low. Entrepreneurs burn-out, run out of money, and/or simply lose their stamina or passion along the way.

For the first few years, most entrepreneurs struggle in a financial roller-coaster ride between feast and famine, more frequently with famine winning out. During the ride, it is common that entrepreneurs get stressed out, start questioning themselves, even wonder if their pursuit is putting their personal and financial health in devastation. Some may even wonder if they should quit entrepreneurship and just go back to getting a job, collecting a regular paycheck, and living that old mundane, unfulfilling, but nonetheless more predictable life.

BUT, there is good news. While it is not easy to endure through the first 5 years, there are entrepreneurs who made it! There are many examples of successful entrepreneurs who surpassed their 5th, 10th or even 20th year. They have walked the entrepreneurship journey to create businesses that have changed the way we eat, shop, travel, learn, invest and even sleep!

These successful entrepreneurs weren't just lucky. They walked the same road of adversity and hit many road bumps, even road blocks along the way. They learned from others and leveraged on their resources, however limiting it might be, to build better processes, better teams, better systems every step of the way. Whatever your passion is, whatever business you want to create, crossing that finish line is possible if you seek to understand, learn from your own mistakes, as well as other's mistakes.

I was born into an entrepreneurial family. My six older brothers all owned their businesses, so from a young age, I was able to observe the struggles of life being an entrepreneur up-close. Sleepless nights, long hours, no vacation, no family time, irregular meals, shortage of cash, people problem, you name it, it's all part of the package.

If you think that starting your own business means you will make a lot of money, work 40 hours a week, have a wonderful work-life balance, be chill and stress-free, well, please highlight the next sentence. GO GET A JOB. Entrepreneurship is not for you.

Since young, I have the entrepreneurial blood in me. I knew I wanted to start my own business one day, but after watching my brothers' struggles, I thought I needed to be smarter in my approach. My game plan was to obtain a Master's degree in Business Administration (MBA), get a good job, get paid to learn, and when I'm ready to be an entrepreneur, hopefully I would make less mistakes.

So after obtaining my MBA from University of Chicago, I kick-started my career in Fortune 500 companies and went through a series of leadership trainings, job rotation programs, and experienced first-hand what it meant to run a multi-billion-dollar company. Then I worked backwards into middle market companies (less than a billion dollar in revenue), then into small companies (less than $100 million), before stepping out on my own.

During my corporate career days, I rotated and trained in functions including Financial Planning and Analysis, Treasury, Risk Management, Audit, Operations Finance, and subsequently also led Accounting, Information Technology, Legal, Human Resources, Operations, Sales & Marketing, and other functions. I held C-suite positions at a relatively young age, not to mention being a minority woman, Asian, and immigrant. Many perceived my climb to the top of the corporate ladder as a huge accomplishment, which I should be set for life.

But there was a void in my heart. Something seemed missing. My husband thought it was a mid-life crisis happening 10 years too early. While being engrossed in climbing the corporate ladder and competing in the rat race, I forgot my childhood dream of being an entrepreneur. Perhaps you might feel the same way too. Life is good, why rock the boat? But if you don't take the chance, you would never know. I left the comfort of my C-Suite life in search of my unanswered calling. The rest was history.

As a first-time entrepreneur, I still remembered how exciting, yet scary it was. "Do I have enough money?" "How do I get clients?" "When can I make a profit?" "How do I pay mortgage?" etc etc. These emotional bubbles kept popping up in my head now and then.

The entrepreneurship journey is like a muddy, dirt road, sometimes sprinkled with camouflaged pot-holes. A road less traveled but it could take you to amazing destinations. The path is not for the faint of the hearts. It tests your patience and your courage. It calibrates your endurance through the school of hard-knocks. If you want to graduate, you must persevere.

Being an entrepreneur allows for self-expression and self-evolution. When I was in the corporate world as CEO or CFO, I was able to rely on all the provided resources, a good paycheck, a corner office, and perhaps a reserved parking spot (premium in Los Angeles). However, there were limitations and restrictions by the Board and shareholders as to what I could or could not do. Or what were the corporate objectives and priorities that I should focus on. As an entrepreneur, I have a lot more liberty and freedom. I can instill my value into my own company and evolve my company at my own pace, focusing on what I believe is important. My company is essentially an extension of me, my value, my image. That's why entrepreneurs view their business as their baby. The feeling is understandable.

I have founded and launched several more companies in the past 13 years. I absolutely love being an entrepreneur. At my current company BIC Group LLC, my team and I are blessed to work with many business owners owning start-ups to $100-million-dollar companies. We provide complete back-office support at a fractional cost. Our service includes Accounting, Financial Analysis, Human Resources, Informational Technology, Legal Administration, Board/CEO Advisory. All in a one-stop shop.

With our direct interactions with entrepreneurs, I know how hard, how real the struggles can be, and I have also seen their pot of gold at the end of the rainbow. It is tough no doubt, but it is also liberating and can be wholly fulfilling. Entrepreneurs believes their destiny is in their own hands. They are their own making.

As a serial entrepreneur myself that has beaten the odds of failure, I believe it is important to share my learnings to pay it forward and cultivate a discipleship of entrepreneurs throughout the world.

Education is one of the best tools you can equip yourself to steer towards the positive side of the statistics. In this book, you will gain insights and coaching from successful business leaders. You will read about what works, what doesn't, what to avoid, and what to look out for. Learn from these business leaders' collective successes and mistakes. Avoid the pitfalls they warn you about. I hope each chapter will inspire you to act and to steer your company onto the right track, hopefully encountering lesser road bumps along the way.

It is inevitable that you will face challenges in your business. It is a matter of "when", not "if". Hang your ego at the door and reach out to business coaches and mentors to help you through. Don't stress out by yourself sitting in a cold dark office room alone. There are people who care about you. Feel free to reach out to any of the authors in this book if you want as we are resources for you too.

Chin-Up and embrace the journey.

Angy Chin

CHAPTER 1

THE POWER OF OPEN-SOURCE PEER-REVIEWED DUE DILIGENCE™

By ALEXANDER SONKIN

For many years, we have been made aware of how Mark Zuckerberg, Jeff Bezos, Warren Buffet, and a few select owners of multi-billion-dollar leading companies are paying virtually zero in taxes while hard-working business owners are paying as much as 50% of their income or more.

How is it possible that only a select number of family offices and certified public accountant (CPA) firms that serve these lucky billionaires have figured out what the rest of the traditional tax planning community seems unable to comprehend? How come the largest, most well-known CPA firms, law firms, and family offices are unable to access the best ideas and deliver comparable results to their clients?

The answer: Due diligence as it pertains to sophisticated tax planning is very challenging, time consuming, and risky. Traditional firms simply do not have access to the leading specialists, time, or energy to do it proficiently. They are overwhelmed with just producing their tax returns and financial statements. Bezos, Zuckerberg, Buffet, and a few others are using non-traditional Family Offices that are supercharged by elite income tax mitigation specialists to win big in the tax game, where the vast majority of their competitors are taking large, avoidable losses.

The US Tax Code is one of the world's most complicated legal documents, with over 150,000 pages and counting, and nobody seems to know how many pages are actually there. The tax planning due diligence process is multi-faceted and involves: 1) accessing new forward-thinking ideas/solutions that mitigate future tax liabilities, 2) analyzing the relative benefits and costs, 3) comparing them to the universe of other potential solutions, 4) analyzing which ideas will best support the clients' specific set of goals, and 5) most importantly analyzing the risk of a possible audit or tax court.

Tackling the due diligence process successfully involves building a non-traditional system that enables thought leaders and specialists from around the world to work together, so they can share their wisdom and bounce ideas off of one another. Traditional CPA Firms, Law Firms, and Family offices are simply not interested in taking the necessary steps to implement this mind-sharing system, because they were designed to operate as private, competing storefronts.

A revolutionary and disruptive solution that originated from the same technological advances that enabled companies like Amazon, Uber, and Google to organize resources and deliver solutions or services in an ultra-convenient, revolutionary way that would radically change the way we live. For over two decades, THE DUE DILIGENCE PROJECT™, organized by the Virtual Family Office (VFO)Hub, has been attracting an Independent, Open-Source Community of hundreds of elite CPA Firms, Family Offices, Law Firms, and Best-in-Class (Peer-Reviewed) Resources™ that work collectively to make every aspect of the due diligence process infinitely more efficient, effective, while eliminating traditional risk and time constraints.

Tax professionals who are given exclusive access to participate in THE DUE DILIGENCE PROJECT™ (DueDiligenceProject.com)can not only compete with but are able to dominate much larger 'Old Big Brand CPA Firms' who are stuck using the outdated traditional due diligence systems, which have proven ineffective.

The smallest CPA firms in the middle of rural America that have discovered this innovation are delivering 10 times to over 100 times the value than the best-known brand name firms. So, let's take a deep dive into the details of what is really happening.

Why Is the Current Due Diligence System for Sophisticated Tax Planning So Mysterious and Broken?

Before the technological revolution began to change how and where we work in the 1990s, the very brightest and best were comfortable taking W-2 jobs at Deloitte, KPMG, and Goldman Sachs, among others. But everything changed over the next two-and-a-half decades. The best and brightest left those big, boxy firms, set up their own smaller, specialized companies, made their own rules, and lived where they wanted. Now these big, brand name firms, who were once employing the best and brightest, are left with people who are still willing to be W-2 employees... not the very best. According to the IRS, 1099 filings have increased by 22% from 2000 to 2014, while W2s have only grown by 2% over that time period.

As one of the original founders of THE DUE DILIGENCE PROJECT™, I see many former CPAs from Deloitte, KPMG, and EY join the Virtual Family Office Hub as CEOs of their independent firms, so they can access and contribute to the wisdom and vetting process that exists inside this exclusive community of thought leaders.

The traditional due diligence process for sophisticated tax planning has been kept very private and mysterious. Every firm talks about doing due diligence, but how do they really do it? Finding new ideas and vetting them properly (for audit or tax court risk) takes an enormous amount of time, energy, and specialized resources.

The due diligence process is multi-faceted and involves the following three aspects:

- **a.** Accessing new ideas, resources, and specialists
- **b.** Fully vetting those ideas, resources, and specialists
- **c.** Successfully implementing those ideas into real-life plans while mitigating risk.

Working with hundreds of elite CPA firms, law firms, and specialists who were invited to participate in the DUE DILIGENCE PROJECT™ over the years, has enlightened us as to how traditional firms truly manage their mysteriously private due diligence processes. Our findings were quite shocking.

Financial giants like Deloitte, KPMG, EY and Goldman Sachs, along with their smaller counterparts are not interested in working together with one another to share ideas and participate in a global due diligence initiative. They operate as competing storefronts at a strip mall with private, closed backrooms that are filled with "products" they want to sell to customers.

These "closed storefronts" do not want their customers knowing what their competitors are offering. They want to keep outside ideas and competitors away from their best clients (out of fear of losing them). They keep these clients inside their closed systems, selling them the "approved products and strategies" that are sitting in their private back rooms. They train their people to only sell what they have and to respond 'negatively' to any idea that originates from outside their firm. This way, they don't have to invest in the due diligence process. Since they don't have access to the best and brightest, the real risk is what would happen if they approve a new idea and they are wrong?! They simply cannot afford to take that risk!

Traditional CPA firms are asked to do so much and are stretched too thin just trying to produce a compliant tax return or financial statement, leaving them few resource to make significant changes to their business model. Many CPAs are inundated with smaller clients who generate very little revenue for them and take up a lot of their resources. None of them actually know how many pages are in the tax code, as it is constantly changing, growing, and becoming more complex. They don't have access to the leading resources to effectively do proactive tax planning for their clients.

It takes a lot of time and more importantly access to leading expert specialist in each area to vet a new strategy, and most CPA firms don't have the resources to do this effectively. And, at the end of all their analysis, what if they are wrong? It is much easier for them to say they did due diligence and are "not comfortable" with a particular tax mitigation strategy. They simply recommend the same strategies that everyone else is doing that they already understand.

Tax attorneys who specialize in specific sections of the tax code and actually discover or develop solutions are prohibited by law to market or share what they have discovered publicly. So, how would a CPA or family office CEO who has a client with a significant tax problem even know about this solution unless they met that exact tax attorney? And even if they did meet, without building a strong, trusting relationship, the referral risk of sending their largest clients to a third-party attorney would be too prohibitive.

Financial advisory firms and mergers and acquisition firms are not trained or educated in sophisticated tax planning and essentially have no way to measure the risk or reward of such planning. They typically call their local estate planning attorney who most likely only knows how to sell basic trusts for simple estate planning needs that some other attorney designed.

Amazon is forcing countless retailers to close down many of their storefronts, including Toys-R-Us, Macy's, JC Penny and even Wal-Mart because they are laser-focused on perfecting their customers' experience instead of focused on maximizing profits and keeping their clients in the dark. Customers want transparency, peer-reviewed feedback, efficient process, and confidence when they make a decision. This trend is now beginning to take form in the tax planning universe, as more sophisticated business owners are leaving their traditional CPAs for proactive Tax Professionals who have are more focused on bringing new ideas and enhancing the customer experience, as opposed to selling more tax returns and financial statements.

Let's look closely at how their Best-in-Class (Peer-Reviewed) Products and Services can be quickly vetted by customers to create massive time savings, confidence, and cost savings, making it impossible for storefronts to compete. Even Wal-Mart, who was once thought of as a virtual monopoly is feeling the Amazon pressure and they will have to make massive changes or they will be "Amazoned" out of business as well.

The proactive tax planning due diligence revolution is disruptive, bringing world-class tax planning solutions to millionaires that were recently only available to a few lucky billionaires!

The Solution Is Simple, Elegant, and Obvious

Essentially, when we look at storefronts with back rooms, we see the old outdated business models of Toys-R-Us, JC Penny, and malls that are closing down around the country. Those companies did not change their business models and they are no longer valuable in the marketplace when comparing them to Amazon. These dinosaurs were focused on themselves while Amazon was focused on the customer.

When we look closely at traditional Wall Street firms, large CPA firms, law firms, and wealth management firms, their business models resemble Toys-R-Us much more than they resemble Amazon. They are so focused on themselves that they don't even remember why they are doing what they do in the first place.

They key is to focus on the customer experience and what their ideal customer actually wants, which is:

- **a.** Confidence that they are working with people who have the best ideas and the best resources on the planet
- **b.** Time savings in that they can make one phone call to one point of contact who can deliver them best in class solutions.

This is exactly what Amazon has figured out how to do better than any other company in the world.

How can we apply Amazon's amazing success to the multi-trillion-dollar financial services industry and bring efficiency and effectiveness to hard working families and business owners who want someone to trust with their most-important financial matters, including proactive tax-planning?

The Amazon-inspired solution that is fully disrupting the entire financial services industry and is bringing Best-in-Class (Peer-Reviewed) Resources™ to family offices and elite CPA firms is a company called the Virtual Family Office Hub, a unique global community of Best-In-Class Resources™ supporting elite CPA firms, family offices, and law firms who serve successful business owners and families.

Elite CPAs, Family Office Leaders, and Tax Attorneys who want to stay relevant in the Economic Ecosystem of the Future™ have a unique opportunity to participate in THE DUE DILIGENCE PROJECT™ (DueDiligenceProject.com). Those who qualify will also have access to the Virtual Family Office Hub (VFOHub.com), where they can access a global network of Best-in-Class (Peer-Reviewed) Resources™ and sophisticated, vetted strategies that have been only available to elite billionaire families. Participating firms can now deliver world class results in the form of significant tax and cost savings that have a profound effect on their clients' net worth, quality of life, and ability to impact their communities.

Toys-R-Us felt the pressure of Amazon coming and they had time to adapt. Because they were too focused on themselves and NOT what their customers actually wanted, they chose to stay the course and keep doing what every other storefront operator was doing.

What The VFO Hub and THE DUE DILIGENCE PROJECT™ has accomplished over a few decades is to organize the first open-source, peer-reviewed platform of independent law firms, CPA firms, family offices, specialists, and Best-In-Class Resources™ into one global community that continues to grow and attract the very best. This snowball is gaining momentum in terms of size, quality, experience, and execution while its big, boxy, outdated competitors don't even know why they are losing some of their most high-profile clients.

An elite CPA or Tax Attorney or Specialist who qualifies to participate in THE DUE DILIGENCE PROJECT™ through the Virtual Family Office(VFO)Hub Global Community is able to:

- **a.** Access cutting edge wisdom, completed due diligence and education on key strategies and concepts that have been vetted by independent peers who include elite CPAs, tax attorneys, specialists, and thought leaders from around the world.
- **b.** Contribute additional, independent feedback to the ongoing due diligence analysis that has already been completed by hundreds of independent, participating firms.
- **c.** Access uniquely, custom-designed solutions from combined strategies that were created through collaborative brainstorm sessions within our global community.
- **d.** Deliver world class tax mitigation solutions or a custom designed Virtual Family Office Experience - Supercharged by Best-in-Class (Peer-Reviewed) Resources™ & Specialists

THE DUE DILIGENCE PROJECT™ is Helping Successful Business Owners Win Like Never Before

We are seeing small, local CPA firms to utilize this accelerated due diligence system to deliver vetted solutions that, in one case, saved a client over $17.5 million in unnecessary taxes. The competing local advisor who worked for a global wealth management/mergers and acquisitions firm, which generates almost $38 billion in revenues, designed a plan that saved this client only $3 million. What is most embarrassing about this real-life situation is that the $38 billion-firm actually had the opportunity to see the plan design of their much smaller competitor. But because the idea did not come from them, they decided to offer their own plan even though it delivered 83% less value to the client. Although this is shocking, it is pretty much par for the course!

Another small CPA firm located anywhere in the United States that was plugged into this disruptive due diligence system saved one of their clients over $3 million in taxes on the sale of an appreciated asset and then helped them invest those tax savings to create an additional $6 million in wealth. Much larger CPA firms and law firms have never even been exposed to those strategies.

A CPA firm who had very few "ideal" clients (when they initially plugged into the Hub) has now decided to fire a client paying over $120,000 per year because they don't want to do the busy work that it takes to earn that revenue. They are making a lot more money delivering massive value to their other clients where they can use Best-in-Class (Peer-Reviewed) Resources™ to do the work.

We are seeing very successful business owners leaving large CPA firms and multi-family offices because they inherently feel that there must be a better solution out there. These "ideal" clients have intuition and understanding that if Zuckerberg and Bezos have teams of advisors who can help them deliver massive value, then there must be someone who can do the same for them, too.

Our way of life is being affected by technological disruptions and innovations. Uber, Amazon, and now VFO Hub have changed the way we travel, purchase products, and handle complicated due diligence to legally minimize our taxes in this new and ever-changing world.

For more information, you or your most trusted tax advisor should visit **www.DueDiligenceProject.com**, **www.vfohub.com** or email **info@vfohub.com**.

CHAPTER 2

THE ENTREPRENEURIAL MINDSET

By **ALEXANDER CHRISTIAN SWIGER**

I don't see entrepreneurship as a career choice. I see it as a mindset. An entrepreneurial mindset is about trying to build the airplane while you are flying it. You can plan the departure and chart the course, but the flight might not be as smooth as anticipated. Unexpected turbulence may show up along the way. How we handle the turbulence isn't always perfect, but we must always continue to learn and develop new skills in order to adapt to our ever-changing environment. I have failed far more times than I have succeeded, but this is just a part of being an entrepreneur.

My entrepreneurial path began on a trip to Las Vegas during my junior year at the University of Southern California. I was majoring in Business Communication, but like many college students I did not know what I wanted to do or what industry I wanted to enter once I graduated. What I did know was that if I worked hard opportunity would arise. I was president of the Communications Honor Society, a member of Lambda Pi Eta honor society, and a liaison to the Dean of the Annenberg School for Communication and Journalism. I also took part in extracurricular activities and attended many events, all the while waiting patiently for my opportunity.

The opportunity that I had been waiting for presented itself on a weekend trip to Las Vegas. My friends and I were having a drink at the Circle Bar in the Hard Rock Hotel and Casino when the bartender gave us passes to the annual Nightclub & Bar Show at the Las Vegas Convention Center.

At the convention center, I walked the expo floor. I struck up a conversation with a gentleman at one of the soda booths. He immediately struck me as an interesting character and reminded me of Richard Branson, the founder of the Virgin Group. His name was Peter Van Stolk and he was the CEO of Jones Soda Co. What stood out to me about his sodas were the unusual flavors, like Green Apple and Blue Bubblegum.

We ended up talking for three hours. I told him I lived in Los Angeles and he said he needed someone in that region. While my friends were enjoying several libations, I walked directly into my opportunity by chance. I arrived home from that Vegas trip with a position as the Jones Soda Area Manager for Southern California.

It was not until after I accepted the job that I realized I did not have any beverage experience or sales and marketing skills. I turned to my older brother, Frank. Like all five of my older siblings, he was always a role model. Lucky for me, he was in the beverage industry at the time. His over-the-phone crash course in beverage product management can be summarized as, "act confident and overcome objections with passion and knowledge." He advised me to let my youth and exuberance stand out more than my lack of experience and knowledge. He also told me to position soda on the shelf or in the icebox at eye level so it is the first thing a potential customer sees.

At 19-years-old I showed up for my first day of work at the Snapple distribution warehouse scared. My job was to pitch Jones Soda to 55 representatives who provided territory coverage from San Diego to LA and accompany this group of 40- and 50-year-old beverage professionals who were mainly focused on selling and distributing Snapple. I learned the business by jumping in their cars, spending the entire day running their established routes, and presenting my product. We went to grocery stores, liquor stores and delis. I would represent Jones Soda while they had a whole portfolio of other beverages to sell. Several months into my job the Jones Soda sales started skyrocketing.

I quickly learned that I represented the lion's share of the Jones Soda case volume sales in southern California. The sales distributors I worked with only cared about pushing Snapple. At the time, Snapple was the hottest, bestselling drink in the beverage industry. It basically sold itself.

During this time, I also learned that the goal of the beverage distribution business is not to stop in a store and sell one product, but to sell as many products as possible there. You need to make that stop as profitable as possible. When I saw that the other reps were only pushing Snapple, I thought "Wow, they are really missing something by just focusing on one product. They are going for the easy sale, but they are leaving a lot of money on the table by not selling the entire portfolio."

I spent two years working my way up in Jones Soda during college. It was a great company to teach me the entrepreneurial ropes. I exceeded every assigned sales quota. I expanded my distribution network from 20 to 100 wholesale companies. By the time I graduated,

I was working with several distributors in multiple states. I saw how much products like Snapple and AriZona ice tea were selling. I also recognized I was doing most of the selling of Jones Soda. Frustrated with the reluctance of Southern California's traditional distributors to consider our product, I went to Peter with my idea to create a new age beverage distribution company using Jones Soda as our flagship brand.

I told Peter that we needed to look into getting some venture capital together. I remember saying to him, "If you give me four vans and four guys, I will teach them how to sell the soda." Peter Strahm, Jones Soda's East Coast sales manager, said to me, "Alex, you are building the airplane while you fly it. How are you going to store the product, how are we going to ship product to you?"

Determined to get my new business venture off the ground I went out to find investors, starting with my inner circle. With the investment money from my eventual father-in-law Marc Nathanson, Cable Pioneer, and Forbes 400, I was able to raise the capital needed to secure a small public storage facility near the Los Angeles International Airport and three vans. I am forever indebted to my original investors for turning over more than $1 million in investment money to an inexperienced kid who relied on bravado and a cocky, fearless attitude. With the graces of Jones Soda and the investment made by my father-in-law, I started my own distribution company called Bottoms Up Beverage Distributor in May 1999, just as I was graduating from college.

I hired Reynaldo Lopez, a distributor from Anheuser-Busch, as my first employee. He taught me the way to execute at the store level and it was his superior training he had received from Anheuser-Busch that proved beneficial in determining our exponential success in the trade. We began product distribution with one Ryder rental truck and leased Econoline vans. Despite building the plane while flying, we grew rapidly. Two years later, Snapple of Southern California acquired Bottoms Up Beverage's assets and distribution rights. At the time, we were the largest exclusive non-alcoholic beverage distributor of Jones Soda in Los Angeles County.

Under my leadership those three initial employees turned into a team of 30 employees. We went from distributing just Jones Soda to also selling Welch's and Langer's juices and Hansen's Signature Soda. In addition to selling beverages to small mom-and-pop stores, we also sold to regional and national superstars like the convenience stores 7-11, AM/PM, Chevron and supermarkets Ralphs and Albertsons. Our sales went from $25,000 a month to a projected $475,000 a month. The more product we sold, the more we had to inventory and eventually finance. This put a terrible strain on Bottoms Up and we needed to be infused with $10 million in investment capital. The ownership and members of the board decided to liquidate the assets. I had successfully built the airplane while I was flying; I was a true entrepreneur.

Looking back, I attribute most of what made me successful in sales and marketing was because my lack of experience. I had no fear. I've learned that as we gain experience, there is a tendency to become our own biggest obstacle. What I learned was I had an unique opportunity to learn how to sell new products in a "rubber meets the road," ground level and grow a product where we could do millions of dollars' worth of sales. In football terms, I had out-kicked my punt coverage.

With Bottoms Up Beverage behind me, I took the same approach of "building the plane while flying" to Wine Warehouse. At the time, they were the largest distributor of wine in country. I met with Jim Myerson, the CEO. He is not only a fearless leader, but a highly educated, wonderful human being. I asked him how I could be of value to his company. He told me to replicate the same model of success I achieved selling Jones Soda and create my own position at his company. I asked what they wanted me to focus on.

"We sell wine, and we have people selling beer and spirits" he told me. "But we hardly sell anything that is non-alcoholic."

I was hired as the California Non-Alcohol Division Brand Manager. I am happy to say that in the eight years of being with Wine Warehouse, I truly loved what I did and the people I worked with. My boss, Ed Rose, helped hone my unpolished approach to business.

I was in charge of bringing in new brands. I had a handle on anticipating the next hot item because I knew the industry and I knew what people wanted. I looked for brands that coincided with health crazes going through the country. Customers were looking for all-natural ingredients and beverages that were not loaded with sugar. I was responsible for bringing in IZZE, an all-natural sparkling fruit juice. I also added FIJI Water and Republic of Tea to the portfolio when they were new and unknown. The brands I brought on complimented Wine Warehouse's wine, spirit, and beer portfolio, as well as the current customer base of restaurants, hotels and grocery store chains. During my time, I grew the non-alcohol portfolio revenues to nearly $10 million.

I often look back to see how my view of success has changed. Twenty years ago, my definition of success was measured by a different scale. I equated success and happiness to monetary wealth and popularity. Today I value what can never be purchased or acquired by monetary success. Success for me is the ability to never give up and never accept failure. Turbulence is only temporary. Today, at 42 years old, I can anticipate turbulence and I know how to calibrate to achieve the desired outcome. We all must take ownership of our actions. Often it is how we react which determines whether we succeed or fail.

I try to take pride in everything I do. I put forth my best effort and know that it is through the failures I have come to appreciate the successes. I never take anything, anyone, or any opportunity for granted. As the late, great tight end for the Oakland Raiders, Todd Christensen, once said, ingratitude is the greatest sin of all.

I consider myself a success on many levels that certainly won't gain acclaim or have me featured in the Forbes 400. Although we all shoot for achievement and goals, what matters most to those who are on that prestigious list, and what I now understand they consider true achievement and success, is having the right mindset and a burning desire to never give up. To act as a true leader who inspires and always continues to learn from their mistakes and willing to learn from others. Today I was a success, but I know tomorrow will bring unexpected challenges and turbulence to my flight that I must overcome. I know I'm prepared for any turbulence sent my way. I know I won't hesitate to ask for advice or seek a second opinion. Today was a good day I will go to bed with a smile on my face knowing I put forth my best effort, that I made an impact on those around me and that impact was positive and filled with love. I hope the insight I have provided will help you go to bed with a smile on your face.

CHAPTER 3

EMPOWERMENT TO DRIVE ACCOUNTABILITY

By **ANGY CHIN**

Starting and growing a business seems simple. Create a product or service that you think people want to buy. Sell that product. As business grows, hire more people, stock more products, sell more, hire more people, and repeat. If it were that simple, then why do half of small businesses fail within their first five years?

For three decades, I have worked with Fortune 500 to middle market to startup companies, helping them evaluate and resolve day-to-day pain points. While business models, processes, and complexities may differ greatly depending on the company's size, the #1 shared challenge of all businesses is people issue.

Do I have the right people? People issue may seem simple and straight-forward, but in my point of view, it's the most difficult part of running a business. Many entrepreneurs say to me, "If only I had the right people, then my business would thrive!" But what does "having the right people" really mean? What kind of people are the "right people?"

There are many books about talent management and how to find the "right people." I am not undermining their importance. However, in this chapter, let's view it from a slightly different angle. Instead of asking "How do I find the right people?", how about asking "How I can be the right boss?"

I grew up in an entrepreneurial family. My six older brothers all became entrepreneurs at a very young age gaining their experience through the school of hard-knocks. Besides viewing their struggles first-hand, my decades of working with entrepreneurs allowed me to observe up close the rewards and challenges of business ownership.

Entrepreneurs live and breathe their business day-in and day-out. Their business is their baby. Sometimes, the level of passion and emotional investment is so deeply rooted that it becomes hard to stay clear-minded and objective. Consciously or subconsciously, most entrepreneurs have a fear of letting go and losing control.

"If I delegate it, will my employee screw things up?" "Will he get it done on time?" "Will she meet my standard?" Add on top the time constraints--no time to train, no time to explain... "Well, perhaps it's better and faster that I just do it myself." Does that sound familiar?

As a result of this mindset, entrepreneurs usually end up being bogged down by day-to-day tasks, work around the clock, with little time off to spend with family or friends. No holiday, no time to stay in bed even when sick, no hobby, no social life, and sometimes no money (all assets invested in the business), and that becomes the accepted way of life. Welcome to the Entrepreneur's Club!

Working this way during startup is inevitable. It is the first step in the entrepreneurship journey. Nonetheless, if it's over a prolonged period, it not only puts strain on the entrepreneur's health and relationships, it also puts the entrepreneur on the fast track to total burnout. Hence, besides running out of money, burnout (as in mental fatigue and physical exhaustion) is one of the top reasons why businesses fail within their first five years.

In order to survive and to scale for the long run, entrepreneurs need to build a team. Not just any team, but a high impact team that is empowered to drive accountability and result. In order to build a team, you need people. So back to my earlier comment. Instead of asking "How to find the right people?" let us discuss "How can I be the right boss to recruit and to retain my people?"

1. Acknowledge the fear of losing control.

First is to admit your fear of losing control. Admission is the first step to healing. You cannot fix what you are not aware.

Next, take a deep breath and write down a list of repetitive and routine tasks that you currently do and the potential consequences if not done exactly the way you want at the get-go. Note how you can spot-check initially before you gain confidence and comfort with not doing it yourself.

2. Accept the fact that no employee is perfect.

In the entrepreneur's eyes, no employee can be perfect. No one can do a job as good as you. You will always be the best person to do the work exactly the way you want it. Others doing what you envision will always be a hit or a miss. That said, if you are waiting for that perfect employee to appear before you delegate, then you may wait for a lifetime. If so, keep your business small to the extent that you can manage it all by yourself and be content. However, if you desire to grow your business, you must learn how to let go, and when to let go.

Seek the greatest strengths in your employees; don't keep focusing on their shortcomings. The truth is that their weakness will never become their strength. Coach them to do what they are best at and use their strengths to support you. Help them sharpen their skills and provide regular feedback for continuous improvement.

Do not assign tasks randomly out of your own convenience without considering the strengths and weaknesses of who you are delegating the tasks to. Being the right boss does not mean delegating blindly. It requires understanding your employees' strengths and weakness in order to maximize their chance of success. Their success is your success.

3. Work on your business, not in your business.

When the company is small, working in the business is the norm. I call it "CEO by day, janitor by night." Nonetheless, at some point during the growth trajectory, you must evolve out of daily firefighting to make time for strategic thinking. Working on the business requires quiet time for big picture thinking, long-term planning, and forecasting in order to achieve sustainability.

For example, a warehouse owner who unloads trucks, tracks down lost shipments, and enters invoices into QuickBooks is working in the business. Whereas building corporate infrastructure, evaluating capital needs, assessing channel expansion, developing new partnership are associated with working on the business.

If your goal is to grow, you must evolve out of working in the business to working on the business. Such evolution is only possible if you have a trusted team to take over in-the-business tasks.

4. Are you the bottleneck?

You have big dreams, but we are all human and have 24 hours a day. No matter how efficient you are, there is only so much you can do even if you don't sleep!

As business expands, as locations and product lines and people are added, there will come a point in which you will max out in terms of time and energy. Then, unknowingly, you become the bottleneck for everything.

Employees wait for you to call the shots before they can act. They don't feel empowered to make any decision because you are the owner. And because they don't make any decision, they also cannot be at fault if something goes wrong.

In the meantime, you are all stressed-out with people zooming in and out of your office with never-ending questions. Your email inbox is flooded with emails like tsunami that never resides. Your table is like a war zone stacked with piles of paperwork waiting for review or signing. Everyone seems to be waiting for you.

I have seen an entrepreneur hires a Controller but still tells the Controller how to book accounting entries even though the Controller is a Certified Public Accountant and the entrepreneur is not. This creates a habit in which the Controller is frequently waiting for the entrepreneur's instruction before he books any entry. Instead of doing the work he is hired and knows how to do, the Controller is now wasting time in the waiting game. Ironically, the entrepreneur complains why the books take so long to close every month!

If such central command and control structure persists, there will always be a bottleneck, like a traffic jam that never clears.

In the past five years, I have worked with many companies, with revenues from $5 million to $50 million. Their organizational structure tends to have the entrepreneur sitting on the top like King or Queen, followed by an army of soldiers below. The organization is flat. Almost everyone reports directly to the entrepreneur. There is little to no middle management team and, even if there were, they hold managerial titles with no power or authority. The entrepreneur still makes all the decisions.

Such an arrangement is not only inefficient and ineffective, it also poses risks to the company. The entrepreneur may not know the intricacies of the matter at hand while being asked to make a decision. They may end up making a decision based on self-perception, hearsay, incomplete or even inaccurate information. If the decision yields poor outcome, the entrepreneur cannot hold anyone accountable as employees' reactions will simply be, "I was just carrying out the owner's order." This type of organizational structure creates a team of human robots or puppets with no sense of empowerment or accountability.

This single command and control mode of operation stifles company growth. If not dealt with promptly, it greatly limits the company's growth potential. In other cases, I have seen companies grow big but then regress to a much smaller size due to costly mistakes made by the entrepreneurs. And in some cases when the entrepreneur dismissed an employee in-charge of the failed project, the employee filed a wrongful termination lawsuit.

Be careful of your behavior. Every action yields an outcome, whether you like it or not.

5. Don't have more direct reports than the number of days you are willing to work.

After you commit to fixing the bottleneck issue, the next question is how to design and build a proper middle management team. Bigger companies have layers of executive and middle management teams, but for the purpose of our discussion, I would generalize them into a single group called the "middle management team" to capture all employees with supervisory and management responsibilities.

Building a middle management team is like building a house. Prior to building a house, you hire an architect to draw a blueprint that aligns with how you like to live and what you like to do. Then, you approve the blueprint before the builder constructs it. The whole process requires deep thinking, pre-planning, foresight, and clear understanding of what you want. The worst thing that could happen is haphazardly going through the planning process, then halfway through the execution, you request major structural changes, not just cosmetic modifications.

Similarly, it is critical to design an organization chart with the proper middle management team to help you realize your business dream. This will be the platform to nurture future leaders for the company. Your success will depend on how well this team is designed.

As a rule of thumb, my advice is don't have more direct reports than the number of days you are willing to work. Since there are seven days per week, seven direct reports would be the max. If you have more than seven direct reports, it would be hard for you to effectively mentor each of your direct reports while still making time to explore more strategic work.

6. Hire tough and train hard.

Having a good job description is the first step to recruiting. It is not just for the sake of complying with the state's labor laws; rather, it is a tool to articulate your expectation for the role. Then comes the interview process.

When helping my clients interview candidates, I quiz the candidates on technical competency and observe their attitudes during the rounds of phone and face interviews. It is key to find someone with the right fit for the company, its culture, and the position. And if the position reports to the entrepreneur, make sure both parties possess the chemistry to work together. Skill set is best to be complementary to prevent group think. Diversity is the best policy.

After hiring, the next step is to train, train, train. This is not just about training on technical skill. It is about coaching and mentoring to help them understand how the business operates, even if the new employee has years of industry and functional experience. Each company has nuances such as management style, communication preferences, and priorities that the employee needs to know in order to become an effective team player.

Once trained, it is time for you to let go and hand over the reins. This is often the toughest time, emotionally-speaking. In my experience, I have seen many entrepreneurs struggled tremendously. The head says, "I am ready to transition", however in reality, the heart resists. Walking the talk is not easy. Saying it and doing it are two very different things.

7. Let them walk.

Like a discipleship program, once the employees are trained, it is important that you get out of the way and let them do their job. Check back to ensure they are ramping up smoothly. This is not about throwing someone to the deepest end of the pool and seeing whether they sink or swim.

I equate this transition to parenting a toddler. When a child is ready to walk, the parents need to back off and let the child walk. The child might stumble and fall at the beginning, but it is OK. Encourage them to get back up on their feet and keep moving forward. Wise parents are the ones who stay by their child's side observing and helping as necessary, not grabbing the child's arms so tightly and walking for them.

When an employee makes a mistake (and they will), coaching is much more effective than reprimanding them. Part of empowerment is allowing them to make mistakes, learn and grow, and move forward.

8. Coach and support them.

Whatever you choose to call yourself, whether CEO or President, being the head of the company requires you to set clear strategic direction for your company. That's your job!

All roads lead somewhere, but it may not be where you want to be. If you cannot articulate your who/what/when/where/how strategic direction clearly, don't expect your middle management team to read your mind and know what you want. Most people do not have ESP (extrasensory perception).

From the strategic direction, your middle management team can then develop their own departmental goals. As long as all the goals supports the same endgame, there will be alignment and reinforcement to drive the company forward. Team spirit will be high, and the sense of purpose will be strong.

Mid-year, sit down and review progress with your middle management team. Take pulse checks consistently. Celebrate accomplishments frequently. Recalibrate carefully. Discover or re-define what else needs to be done. Discuss resource needs, brainstorm how to overcome roadblocks. Being the right boss means being present and engaged. Stop looking at your iPhone during meetings or conversations. Your full attention shows that you care. If they think you don't care, then why should they care?

For the past 20 years, I have also utilized weekly one-on-one and breakfast team meetings as part of coaching and support toolkits. When middle managers can celebrate their ups and downs with one another, there is cross-pollination in learning, and it enhances team spirit. Everyone can learn from each other; they don't just have to learn from the leader. That leads to the next point.

9. Hang your ego at the door.

As a company grows, hire people smarter than you to run the show. That may be a threat to your ego. Unlike the fear of losing control, this is more of a fear of losing status or significance in your own company.

You may ask yourself asking hiring the middle management team, "What role do I play now? What status do I have? If I cannot call

all the shots, then who am I? Will people obey me? Will they respect me? Will I still be perceived as the smartest person in the room?"

Admit it or not, a self-serving ego is often the underlying reason why you adopt a central command and control model and resist having a middle management team. Employee empowerment is not in your dictionary because you want to feel important and needed by making all the decisions. If this is your strong need, then admit it and forget about growing big.

Wise entrepreneurs who want to grow their companies know when to hang their ego at the door. Many successful entrepreneurs admit to the business outgrowing them and, in many cases, choose to fire themselves and hire professional CEOs.

I once met a successful entrepreneur who built three businesses and sold each one of them when they reached $20 million in revenue. He said to me, "I am a $20 million man. When the company reaches that size, I have a hard time managing it. And yet, I couldn't bring myself to hire a professional CEO and sit on the wayside. So, I'd rather sell it and build another one. I enjoy the building process." There is tremendous self-awareness and wisdom in this sharing. This personal insight has led him to three successful exits.

10. Empowerment drives accountability.

When all the above steps are taken, you have exercised the art of empowerment to drive accountability. And with accountability drives results.

Let's play this movie: The entrepreneur tells a department manager that he is fully in charge. Then the entrepreneur adds, "You are in charge and responsible for the result, but before you make any decision, run everything by me first." If you were the recipient of this message, how empowered do you feel? How accountable are you? Are you truly "in charge"? Or is that just a hypocritical comment? And with the entrepreneur frequent travel and slow to respond, when you miss a deadline, who is at fault? Being an employee, is such empowerment real or a sham?

Be the right boss. If you don't like to be in that shoe, don't put your employees in that shoe. Your success, scalability, and sustainability depend on your middle management team. To leap-frog your company forward, every step counts. It is a waste of time, life, and money constantly taking three steps forward and two steps backward.

You have a choice to make. Empower others and see your business soar to new heights or stay small and be happy. Whichever you choose, Chin up!

CHAPTER 4

AN ENTREPRENEUR'S GUIDE TO SURVIVING A BUSINESS IMPLOSION

By **ARMINDA FIGUEROA**

In 2018, I pulled my business back from the brink of implosion. Although it was one of the most challenging times of my life, I emerged from the experience with hard-won managerial skills and a successful business that provides excellent services to clients across the country. My story begins in Puerto Rico where I grew up amid a family with a rich history of entrepreneurism. My paternal grandparents, Carmen and Francisco, owned a gas station where I developed a work ethic and learned how to pump gas, provide outstanding customer service, and manage a business. Neither of my grandparents had graduated from high school, but they managed to provide their two sons with college educations. Paco, my father, and Fernando, my uncle, went on to achieve successful careers in the fields of business and medicine, respectively. Watching them, I saw firsthand how hard work reaped rewards.

My first entrée into the world of entrepreneurism began in the 1970s and continued for over a decade. I set up a candy shop I sold Avon and I sold Amway. Then, with a college friend, we opened a pop-up boutique named Dreams in my mother Arminda's home office. Together, we roamed the streets and shops of New York City's Fashion District buying clothes that we exported back to Puerto Rico.

We sold the curated garments to our friends who could not source the newest trends at their local malls.

I was 22 years old when I graduated from the University of Puerto Rico with a bachelor's degree in business and a minor in marketing. The year was 1987 and the time was right to relocate to New York City. I intuitively knew that the city would provide the classroom I needed to learn how to succeed in business. It was there that I was first introduced to corporate America and where I pursued postgraduate studies. Twenty-nine years ago, my dream city also gave me the best gift of my life: an introduction to my soulmate and wife, Amilda.

During the 1990s and 2000s, I had an amazing climb up the corporate ladder. An old high school friend opened the door for me at Anheuser-Busch, which was my big break. I interviewed and was subsequently hired as marketing coordinator. I was on top of the world! My career there was an education in and of itself. I always say I got my PhD in marketing from A-B University.

After four years on the job, I was appointed Anheuser-Busch's first woman District Manager. Can you imagine? A Latina overseeing five independent or company-owned distributors! My training at Anheuser-Busch armed me with the confidence I needed to win over an angry audience and dissipate a potential boycott of Budweiser products by New York's Latino community. I did this by using my emotional intelligence skills and negotiation skills I learned from a certificate course at the Massachusetts Institute of Technology (MIT) and by leveraging the trust I had earned from the community. This experience propelled me to my next career ascension within Anheuser-Busch. I was selected to serve on a special task force, comprised of twelve executives from across the country, that went to

Mexico to conduct a due diligence study on the feasibility of investing $1 billion in Grupo Modelo, a large Mexican brewery.

I realize now that each and every triumph or defeat was a lesson learned that I would use again later in life. In 2007, I founded Latin2Latin Marketing & Communications (L2L) in Fort Lauderdale, Florida. L2L is a boutique advertising agency, and our niche is assisting corporations and organizations of all sizes to engage with Spanish-speaking consumers. We developed the Latin Ready Assessment®, an online tool that allows executives to determine their ability to create and launch a marketing program that targets Hispanics. The tool identifies strengths and weaknesses and the results lead to the construction of a marketing plan that builds brand awareness and loyalty among Latinos.

My team and I worked very hard. We put our hopes into making the firm successful and financially stable. By 2017, we were on top of our game and I still savor that sweet smell of success and the rush of adrenaline that comes from engaging new clients. I am proud to say that we have worked with leaders from numerous organizations, including PBS, PBS Kids, Scholastic, Mount Sinai Hospital, Lenox Hill Hospital, Northwell Health, OrthoNOW, U.S. Department of Agriculture, KinderCare Learning Centers, MassMutual, UBS, Baylor College of Medicine, and CHI St. Luke's Health–Baylor St. Luke's Medical Center. We billed $2 million in revenue in 2017 and 2018, which represented triple-digit growth. Every day, I welcomed and celebrated the fact that my dreams had finally reached fruition.

However, this is not how the story ends. With success came growing pains among my staff. The seeds of deceit and treason were planted that would propel the company on a downward spiral toward implosion. For me, 2018 will go down as the most challenging year of my professional life. I witnessed the duplicity by those in my company who held the highest positions. One would think that the experiences I had acquired since childhood would have prepared me for what was to come, but they did not.

In the agency's early years, I knew that I could not compete with the larger advertising agencies in the area that paid higher salaries. I amalgamated into our corporate culture practices and policies that would create a work environment that included having fun while "rolling up our sleeves to get shit done." To do this, I crafted a balanced work environment paired with growth opportunities. L2L valued the growth of human interactions just as much, if not more, than business transactions. As the owner, I placed tremendous importance on learning about my employees at a personal level. I believed that by learning about their hopes, fears, and dreams I could provide emotional and fiscal benefits while mentoring them on their career paths. In addition, L2L offered employees flexible schedules that included the ability to work remotely, two weeks of paid vacation, paid sick days, a 401(k) plan, and 17 paid holidays. We also provided team building activities for employees. Our team created a concept we dubbed "romancing the client," which started with our teams taking care of their needs first so that they would be able to entrench themselves in the client's business in order to generate effective strategies reflective of their need while simultaneously building trust and long-term relationships.

Upon reflection, I recognize that my failure to correctly read the warning signs in 2018 caused me to make four grave mistakes in judgement. My myopia was due to three factors. The first was that I give everyone the benefit of the doubt and trust people until proven otherwise. The second was that my focus was solely on growing the company and doubling its size and revenue. The third was our commitment to providing a point of entry into the workforce as a corporate core commitment.

My first mistake was not having a complete succession plan.

Running a multimillion agency requires a solid succession plan that allows for the business to continue without interruption in case the principal dies, gets sick, decides to move on to other projects or resigns. In my case, it is part of my exit strategy to eventually move on to do other projects down the line and not run L2L on a day to day basis. When the agency almost doubled in revenue overnight, I was forced to identify a successor in haste. The succession plan was for my successor to learn the ropes, buy L2L from me, and become president and CEO. Unfortunately, my successor lacked the skills required to handle the pressure associated with managing a multimillion-dollar budget and high-profile clients. As planned, we paired the successor with a senior executive at L2L who was instructed to provide day-to-day coaching and guidance. Sadly, it did not work.

My second mistake involved hiring errors.

Our commitment to providing a point of entry into the workforce resulted in our staff being comprised of an overabundance of inexperienced individuals unable to keep pace in a hyper-growth situation. Further aggravating this deficiency was that the appointed successor's preferred management style created a more relaxed and informal atmosphere amongst staff. Tardiness, task avoidance, elongated food breaks, discussions about what music tracks to include on the daily playlist, nonstop social media interactions, personal text messaging, and other social conversation breaks began to consume a significant portion of the workday. Additionally, the group began to gather socially after work and to travel together, which fostered a hotbed of gossip. Unproductivity combined with a toxic environment caused a vicious cycle; we had to hire more people and were unable to return to our mission of providing jobs for entry-level workers.

My third mistake was blindly trusting people because they had tenure and experience.

The group of individuals I just described were seasoned and experienced. In my mind, they brought a balanced level of maturity, experience, and discipline to the agency to counterbalance the entry-level workers' inexperience. Later, I learned they sabotaged the agency by creating chaos in the office and interacting with clients behind my back. These unauthorized client communications contained either contradicted approved strategy, blatantly false information, or rumors.

My fourth mistake was that my micro- and macro-visions were not balanced.

I was too busy playing "I made it" and expanding the business to other geographic locations. My day-to-day routine was built around frequent travel to or negotiations with the next big client. As a result, I did not take action quickly enough.

I will spare you the details of my mental health during this six-month period other than it included feeling dazed and defeated and having self-doubt, but also experiencing moments of clarity and awakening. At the end of this process, I was ready to fight back! When I did take action, I found that my learning, experience, and intuition were right. The steps I took I would recommend to other entrepreneurs who are navigating internal and external political strife related to their business. The steps were:

1. **Regroup with Family.** Family can be the most amazing support system imaginable. Go back to basics and consult with your spouse, parents, and siblings on a daily basis each step of the way. While some family members may only provide moral support, others will provide clear strategies for how to overcome situations related to both staff and clients. Remember, I come from a family of entrepreneurs. They reminded me that this was part of the journey and that I would be fine whatever the final outcome may be.
2. **Seek Professional Advice.** One of the best investments I made was to work with an outside business coach and legal counsel. They helped me construct practical strategies that anticipated every conceivable scenario regarding both staff and clients. These strategies were effective and left L2L triumphant.
3. **Cleanse.** Evaluated all options in front of us. We began with an immediate analysis of my firm's financials. Then we implemented austere strategies to prevent financial collapse. We also assessed each staff members' role at L2L. Some staff members left the company, others were let go, and a few chose to stay. This process was painful and shook L2L to its core. Needless to say, a select group of dissidents retaliated and used social media as a weapon to attack L2L by posting defamatory posts and reviews. Although unfortunate, their behavior confirmed that they did not belong at the new L2L.

We also deeply examined each client and assessed the quality of each relationship. I continued the cleansing by firing clients – yes, firing clients--that were no longer a good fit for L2L. Letting go of lack-luster clients actually opened the door for new and amazing projects.

4. **Have Courage.** This became my rallying cry. While having the pluck to clean house and discontinue clients with seven-digit revenue billings was the most frightening decision of my entire business career. It was also the most amazing and liberating feeling I have ever experienced in my career. This process of purging the bad apples within my staff and client roster allowed me to see the souls of the team that would stay with me and get clear about the type of teammates we would welcome to L2L.

Our work to right the ship was validated in 2019 when national brands approached us to help them deliver new strategies and former valued clients returned with new initiatives for us to join. Teamwork, commitment, tenacity, and hard work combined to bring L2L its most important renaissance since its founding.

I know now that everything I went through was for a reason. It also identified for me the people I need in my life to give me the strength to overcome adversity, embrace change, and to move forward with dignity. The key life lessons of this experience included:

- To pay attention to the clues
- Address issues fast and furiously, don't let it fester
- Less is more
- Seek out and engage personally and professionally with individuals (employees/client partners/business associates and friends) who display emotional intelligence, courage, impeccable integrity and share your commitment to growth

- Celebrate total transparency and share the good the bad and the ugly with care and sensitivity
- Pick one trusted person to aid you regardless of need
- Never ever let anyone put you down
- Don't believe the saying "Keep your friends close and your enemies closer"
- Purge all toxic relationships in your life
- Take your time to engage a new client or hire someone
- Conduct your due diligence in business and include an assessment of the other persons character.
- If you feel uneasy move along to the next opportunity
- Love what you do and have fun doing it

I can never thank Renzo, Juanin, Enrique, Michelle, Michael, Malule, Nilda, Jill, my mom Arminda, my spouse Amilda, my dad Paco, and my sisters Carmen and Marie, my business coach Dick Clark and my legal counsel Jose Nolla enough for their support and belief in me and L2L.

CHAPTER 5

SEVEN BEHAVIORAL COMPETENCIES THAT SEPARATE TODAY'S SUCCESSFUL CEOS FROM THE PACK

By **GAIL TOLBERT**

I suppose it would be cliché to say that I have been around the proverbial human resources block for many years (more than I'd like to admit). During my career climbing the rungs on the professional ladder as a human resources expert in fast-paced, fast-growing software companies, I've had the privilege to work closely with a wide variety of CEOs.

Now, I'll admit, it hasn't always been a match made in heaven, and sometimes I crashed and burned. Enter the Story of the Duplicitous CEO.

The Story of the Duplicitous CEO

Let me start by saying that there is a reason the phrase "Don't judge a book by its cover" sticks around. Some years ago, I was hired by a particular CEO to grow and develop a global human resources (HR) department for a company that had switched its business model from a profitable professional services firm to a start-up software development company, taking on venture capital money for the first time.

The interview process went by faster than the speed of light, with a phone call, interview, and offer for the position taking place all in the same day. I'll admit that I was swept off my feet and excited and opportunistic about my ability to be successful in the role. It's what I refer to now as the honeymoon period of my relationship with a new company. The CEO was funny and engaging and the CFO was approachable and easy to get along with. I thought to myself, Finally! An organization with leaders who I trust and respect, will support my role, and seem to be well-liked by employees. And, to top it off, they have a solid board of directors along with known investors in the marketplace who will provide guidance as the company grows... Awesome!

I'm not sure of the exact moment when my fairy tale of a story started to lose its bedazzled charm, but I'm fairly confident it happened pretty quickly after I started. As any good HR leader would do, I set out to develop relationships inside the organization to build trust and allow me to be effective at implementing future changes to the company to meet its growth needs. I met with various groups of employees and asked for feedback on what was and was not going well in the organization. At first, I listened to just the run-of-the-mill challenges, such as complaints about compensation increases that were committed to verbally but never came, issues with ambiguous or nonexistent bonus plans, and unfulfilled promises of promotions. Then I began to listen to feedback about the CEO's obvious favoritism of certain employees, his retention of unqualified "friends and family of the CEO" in leadership positions, and his leadership style of micromanaging, which ironically drove out members of the leadership team who were actually qualified to do the job just about as fast as they came in, most involuntarily.

Then there was a reorganization that involved layoffs, in which I would describe as a process that was not strategic or well-thought-out in my humble opinion. What started out as a fair and objective process of deciding who would have to be let go quickly fell apart as the CEO undermined the decisions of his leadership team. He made changes to the layoff list up to the very last minute that made absolutely no sense and put us in a liable position. The layoffs were executed horribly and, quite honestly, it was a real morale buster. Yes, I was frustrated because I should have been empowered to lead that process, but the rug was pulled out from under me and I was left to clean up the mess.

It was quite apparent at this point that the CEO was incredibly talented at painting an entirely different picture for the board than the actual reality of day-to-day operations. Let's just say that I knew at this point that my future at the company was questionable at best. And then came the straw that broke the camel's back: every HR leader's worst nightmare come true, the day that they accidentally find out that an unethical relationship is happening underneath their nose. Don't worry, the nightmare didn't last long. Word made it round to the CEO that I was aware of his intimate relationship with the CFO , who was not only the CEO's direct report, but more importantly, it violated the checks and balances process put in place in order to make sure the company's finances were never compromised. This set the clock in motion. Tick tock, tick tock. Did I also mention that he was married? Sorry, I digress. The next day I received an ambiguous text from the CFO with an invitation to a meeting that afternoon with her and the CEO. When I inquired as to what the meeting was concerning, I got no response. The time of the meeting kept changing throughout the morning, and at this point my Spidey senses were on full alert.

As I came back from lunch with other members of my team and settled down at my desk (at the time I was sharing an office with my recruiting manager), the scene was set. I swear it was just like out of the movies. The way our desks were situated in the office left it so that our backs were to each other. We both started to log on to the system, but access was denied. We were both banging on our keyboards, trying to figure out what was wrong with the network. Then it hit both of us at the same time. We turned around and looked at each other and knew it was over.

Almost instantaneously the CFO showed up at our door and requested my presence in the boardroom. I don't need to explain the sordid details of the next 30 minutes, but suffice it to say that I was out of a job, based on a falsified termination with cause accusation. And then, to add insult to injury, my recruiting manager was terminated for no reason within minutes and neither one of us with pay. Don't worry, we drowned our anger and sorrow in margaritas and simultaneously decided to celebrate by taking out our to-do lists and ripping them to shreds. I'll admit, it was a freeing moment.

I tell you this verifiably true story of a job gone bad to show you an example of what it is like to work for the opposite of an ethical CEO. Truth be known, all my past professional experiences, good and bad, opened the door for me to gain a deeper appreciation of and respect for the many complexities, pressures, and challenges of the CEO role. I imagine it is similar to having to juggle multiple balls in the air, maybe even for the first time, and never knowing exactly how many you will have to juggle on a given day. Oh, and did I mention that everyone is counting on you not to drop a single one?

Each CEO I worked with either directly or indirectly taught me invaluable lessons about leadership. These lessons have pushed me to become a more effective HR and business professional, to grow more self-aware, and to accept responsibility for how I show up in the world personally and professionally. So, after my experience with the Duplicitous CEO , and several others that followed, I started to think about where I would take my career next, and the idea of continuing to learn from my own and others' leadership experiences while helping CEOs succeed quickly came to mind. And thus my coaching practice was born.

It has been and continues to be a humbling and gratifying experience to not only learn from the past experiences of others, but also to challenge CEOs to embrace the concept that success as a leader comes not only from recognizing and building on strengths, but also from taking the risk of practicing vulnerability with their teams. What I mean by practicing vulnerability is seeing CEOs engaging in open and honest dialogue with their teams about who they are outside of work, their own areas of desired development, sharing examples of past failures as well as lessons learned from those experiences, taking accountability where necessary , and most importantly consistently communicating and supporting the notion that success does not come without failure because embracing failure unleashes and inspires creativity, builds resilience and confidence, invites wisdom, and throws dirt in the face of fear. And so I ask, when did it become wrong or seen as a sign of weakness for leaders to portray themselves as anything but powerful and perfect? I'd argue that there is something spectacular that happens when we are able to establish a culture that embraces a failing forward mantra. Leaders that "get it" and practice it consistently, have the ability to impact bottom line results exponentially.

You see, it is not just a great responsibility, but also a privilege to be in a position to lead others. If we are not working to consistently invest in our strengths and development as leaders, how can we expect to inspire our employees and stakeholders to do the same?

So, what seems to be the common thread linking great leaders together in today's workforce? The following are the seven behavioral competencies that I believe are making the most impact.

1. Empowering Others.

Great leaders create opportunities for others to succeed. I'll be blunt: it's not about you. There is no place for ego in the role of CEO. Here is what you can do to empower others in your organization:

- Find the smartest, most talented people possible, then set them loose to create.
- Give people the support to make decisions.
- Spend time consistently developing other leaders. After all, you don't want to do your job forever, do you?
- Intentionally create the right environment to inspire productivity and inspire maximum performance.
- Define what maximum performance means and how you are supporting that effort.
- Make sure your people are engaged in the success of the organization and understand the contributions that they are making toward that success.

2. Integrity and Trust.

Successful leaders live and breathe integrity inside and outside the office doors. To be honest, without it no real long-term success is possible. Strong leaders believe that leadership is both a responsibility and a privilege and that neither can be taken lightly. They know it often takes time to build trust, but that it can be destroyed in an instant. Here are actions you can take that show integrity and build trust:

- Have the courage to do the right thing, no matter what the cost. Always do right by your employees and your customers.
- Commit only to promises you know with 100% certainty that you can keep. Empty promises may serve you in the moment but will invalidate you eventually. Do what you say and say what you do.
- Always be transparent and timely with good news and bad news alike.
- Take accountability. Be forthcoming about your own mistakes instead of making excuses and blaming others.

3. Strong Communication.

Good leaders have a vested interest in always having their finger on the pulse of the organization. They listen and encourage all feedback from all directions. Here are actions you can take that indicate strong communication skills:

- Communicate negative informative by providing context first, then the "what "followed by the "why
- Consistently practice active listening.
- Invite both good and bad feedback from all stakeholders.
- Manage the flow of information.
- Communicate often in a timely way with transparency.

4. Strategic Mindset.

Successful CEOs don't just say that they are strategic: they embody the actions of what it means to be strategic on a daily basis. Having a strategic mindset means putting yourself, your leadership team, and your organization in a position of strength by having to make as few reactive decisions as possible. Here are activities that indicate a strong strategic mindset:

- Clearly define and communicate the long-term vision to everyone in the company with the attitude that the focus is on the journey and not the destination.
- Revisit your organization's mission statement at least once a year to be sure everyone is on the same page.
- Engage the leadership team in a strengths, weaknesses, opportunities, and threats (SWOT) analysis exercise every so often. The frequency with which you do this will depend on your industry and demographics (usually every 6 to 12 months). The purpose of a SWOT analysis is to get managers thinking about everything that could potentially impact the success of a new project. Failure to consider a key strength, weakness, threat or opportunity could lead to poor business decisions.
- Plan for the short-term and the long-term direction of the organization by creating a top-down strategic plan that includes input from every department leader and clearly shows every department's responsibility in reaching the overarching company goal.
- Schedule quarterly check-ins for your leaders to report to you on progress. Hold your leadership team accountable for being present, meeting the objectives, and asking for support when needed.

- Regularly communicate progress on the strategic plan to the entire organization to reinforce accountability.
- Values-Driven. Values and mission statements are at the heart of any organization and when done correctly they can create a stickiness internally, creating loyalty and increased productivity with employees and externally with customers, who feel good about their partnership with a company that has purpose and are therefore less likely to move their business elsewhere . Values make a statement about who works here and what's important to know about the culture. They also define a standard of daily operation and interaction – internally amongst employees and externally to customers, potential employees, and the community. Here are some recommendations on how to successfully implement values in your organization:
- Create values with intention and live by them. Don't just throw a list of values up on the wall so that you can say that you have them.
- Form a project team of representatives from all areas of the organization to lead the value creation process.
- Weave company values throughout the organization in every way from hiring to performance management to daily culture to conflict management to even your offboarding process
- Model company values through words and actions. Bring them to life. As CEO, it is your responsibility to be a role model every day and to lead by example. This will permeate the company values down throughout the entire organization. You can't half-ass it. I promise that your employees will notice.

5. People First Attitude.

Successful CEOs know that people are the most important part of any organization and that it starts and ends with them. It's that simple. Your employees are the most valuable asset your organization has and if your employees do not perceive that they are valued first, then you have already lost the war. Here are examples of actions CEOs can take that put people first:

- Put employees in a position to succeed and give them assignments that work to their strengths.
- Make intentional investments in employees by taking them out of their silos and bringing them together for events such as team building and innovation sessions.
- Show up and be present. For example, make it a habit to practice "walk around management" on a daily basis, by taking the time to get to know the people who are responsible for your company's success. Not only will it give you better insight into the pulse of your organization, but it will also show that you are invested in them as individuals and that you appreciate what they do for the company.
- Seek to find your employees' capabilities and drive them to achieve great things.
- Put in the time it takes to hire the right people. Once they start, onboard them correctly, give them accountability, and then get out of the way and let them perform.
- Invest in employee development. From day one, support each employee regardless of their position within the company. As long as that employee is part of your organization, don't ever stop supporting them. I promise you that you will see the return tenfold, from increased productivity and engagement to the impact on the bottom line.

6. Empathy.

Research shows that empathy links to trust and, if it is not clear at this point, behavioral skills are necessary if you want to build a relatable connection with people, which is instrumental to the success of all good leaders. People don't care what you know until they know that you care. Employees will go to great lengths for leaders who they know have their backs and recognize them as human beings and talented individuals. Here are ways to be characterized as an empathetic leader:

- Listen. I mean, really listen. Acknowledge and validate each individual's situation without making assumptions. Be aware of your own unconscious bias.
- Ask specific questions that let the individual know you are listening and are engaged in the conversation.
- Respond to all emails and voicemails in a timely manner, even the ones you don't want to respond to.
- Don't immediately jump in and try to solve or fix a problem. This takes practice as many leaders are used to just solving the problem. Instead, just support them. Let them ask for help if they need it.
- As you get to know an employee better, start to recognize the best ways to support and respond to that particular individual. Remember that the same approach does not work for everyone.
- Be patient. Building empathy in the workplace takes time, practice, and consistency, so don't expect it to happen overnight.

There is almost no better honor than to be asked to take on a role, such as that of a CEO, that can influence others personally and professionally on such a grand scale. Committing to being a successful leader is a lifelong practice. It is an internal mindset that for some is instinctual, but for others takes a tremendous amount of hard work.

Great leaders come in all different shapes and sizes and vary in their styles. Some are natural-born leaders, some are leaders by way of learning from the school of hard knocks, and some are well-developed leaders who have been coached since day one. What do they all have in common? Successful leaders never stop learning and never stop caring.

CHAPTER 6

SCALING YOUR BUSINESS FOR SUSTAINABLE GROWTH

By **JEFF NEUMEISTER**

Most entrepreneurs and business owners are familiar with the concept of 'scaling a business' in order to effectively grow revenue, reach a larger audience, and positively impact consumers with the products or services their company offers. Even if you are not a business owner, other key players including executives, middle management, and even employees will often identify systems and innovations within their own roles to successfully scale their precious time through delegation and process implementation. Although it can take time to figure out the right systems for your own business, there are a few standardized places to get started.

This chapter will identify five best practices that you can use to scale a business into an enterprise. Not only are these practices that have been recommended for the companies we audit and consult for, but we also practice what we preach by utilizing these methods within our own firm.

Best Practice #1: Establish a Vision of a Scaled Enterprise

Every successful business starts off with an innovative idea. However, as a business gets off the ground, entrepreneurs can become exponentially busier with daily tasks that can quickly consume the finite hours in a day. This naturally leads to the short-term mentality of 'checking boxes' rather than focusing on a longer-term vision. Ultimately, this narrowed vision may cut the lifecycle of growth-fast! Although daily work is important, sometimes stepping back to observe the business can provide valuable insight about where you want to go and how you can develop a pragmatic plan to get there. Setting realistic expectations, incorporating both short and long-term goals, and pursuing continuous innovation within the business are key to sustainable scale and growth.

A Quick Case Study

Fict, Ion, and Associates ("FIA") was a family office management firm that sought dominance in an industry littered with many mid-sized competitors and a few major players. Its founder had a vision to grow the business to become the largest provider in the space. He started with just a few key clients and was able to scale up to four locations with dozens of employees. However, the business stalled after opening its fourth office space and reported rising employee and client attrition rates. While they were doing a great job onboarding new clients and keeping up with sales volume, the business had effectively plateaued.

The reason for FIA's stall in further scaling can be largely attributed to an incomplete and static vision. The founder had taken many steps for growth that were previously proportional and appropriate for the size of the firm, but then ramped up expectations, which mirrored that of a Fortune 500 enterprise. Implementing large-scale projects and protocols in a mid-sized company can not only block growth, but even backfire as the business may be unable to sustain such massive undertakings. A smaller enterprise must be able to maneuver more quickly given its size. Furthermore, it is important to remember that scaling from $500,000 to $4 million is much different than scaling from $4 million to $100 million.

Establishing a realistic vision for your company also includes being able to adapt to changes in the industry and taking the requisite steps to scale. In order to become the largest and most powerful firm in your industry sector, you will often be required to undertake many smaller and more discrete steps to achieve the set milestones. When it comes to executing a large vision, it is important to be realistic about putting a plan into action to move closer to that large vision. In the case of FIA, the firm had sufficient human capital, financing, and client referrals to continue to scale, but the vision and its implementation discounted other important factors, which essentially bottlenecked further growth and expansion.

Best Practice #2: Internal Housekeeping

The second best practice we have found to be essential is setting up a system around bookkeeping and record documentation, along with identifying software applications that can help organize the business. Most startup businesses have the technical skills to succeed in the industry in which they operate. They identified a lack of innovation in a particular area and decided to bring an idea to market. However, if setting up an accounting process is not within their capabilities and feels too overwhelming, there is always the option of working with an accounting firm to help guide the business.

Setting up a bookkeeping and accounting process will create an accountability system around the money coming in and going out of the business. Understanding what makes up a profit and loss (P&L) statement is a business financial basic and should be a high priority on your to-do list. Understanding the P&L is important not only to those actively involved in the business, but also to potential investors, especially if there are plans to take the company public in the future. Although it may seem tempting to skip saving and categorizing business expense receipts, the charges will add up with rapid speed and suddenly you won't know where all of your money went. You can't measure what you don't track!

In addition to setting up an accounting process, developing a record keeping process for your physical and digital files will also help your company get organized. A well-thought-out filing structure will not only help you locate files but will also allow other team members to fill in the gaps when necessary. With the end-goal being time efficiency, a well-structured filing system can lead to streamlined opportunities for delegation to other team members.

Finally, it is necessary to set guidelines and standards for both internal and external communication. For example, using a project management software where team members can collaborate and communicate will elevate transparency within a company. It can provide a snapshot of the business and operations to both executives and other employees and help move projects through implementation to execution.

Knowing what is going on internally is often a sticking point and can quickly become lost in email threads as businesses expand and get busier, which can lead to a barrier between executive leadership teams and staff. Poor communication can be detrimental to the overall health of a business and further serve to hinder its growth. A survey conducted by the Holmes Report, a leading voice in the global PR industry, concluded that lost productivity stemming from poor communication amounts to over $30 billion annually.

Best Practice #3: Reinvestment

Many business owners take profits out of their business in the form of distributions. Sometimes these distributions are needed to pay bills and maintain a lifestyle, which is understandable to an extent. However, reinvesting a portion of profits back into the business is critical for the longevity of startups and it is necessary if you have the intention of scaling. This process increases working capital, allowing companies to grow, achieve higher valuations, attract favorable attention from investors, and avoid incurring further debt.

Unfortunately, reinvestment of funds back into the company does not lead to automatic growth and success. The key is being strategic with the allocation and intentions of those reinvestments, understanding the vision, goals and objectives for the business, identifying the needs and requirements for maintenance and growth, and then responding accordingly.

Every business is unique and therefore reinvestment can take on many forms. Redirecting excess profits back into business operations is a common form of reinvestment and one that can prove extremely beneficial. Improving infrastructure, replacing outdated equipment, streamlining manufacturing processes, enhancing the customer experience, pursuing an effective marketing strategy, and improving your search engine optimization (SEO) can all lead to an increase in profits and a decrease short- and long-term costs.

It is important to keep in mind that reinvestment is also about investing in people. Human capital is the intangible economic value that an employee adds to a company. Undoubtedly, a strong workforce is one of the greatest assets a company has. When employees feel valued, they are happier and more productive. Companies, in turn, enjoy a lower turnover rate and more success as employee skill is directly related to business status, reputation, pace, and growth. It's a win-win situation.

So just how do you cultivate an environment that recognizes and values human capital? The process starts off with creating a well-thought-out hiring process. Hire the right candidates, develop an internal culture that promotes self-improvement and accountability, and encourage teamwork and idea sharing. Maintaining a human resources department that fosters transparency, open communication, and accountability is paramount for a growing company. Initiatives such as training and continuing education, creating safe and comfortable workspaces, offering benefits, and providing fair and respectful wages all help improve employee satisfaction and retention. While it may sound easy, it requires a constant and proactive effort on the part of management and is something that many companies struggle to achieve.

Last, but definitely not least, reinvest in yourself. Business is a dynamic process and it is important to recognize the value of your time and of the role you play in guiding your company. Find opportunities to improve your own knowledge and skills, whether that be through coursework, certificates, self-help management books, or interactive coaching retreats. Outsource administrative tasks appropriately to free up time for yourself. This allows you the chance to re-evaluate the business, set goals for the future, and strategize how to achieve the outcomes you want. And lastly, never underestimate the power of networking. Building and maintaining relationships can significantly impact the success of your business.

Best Practice #4: Leverage Effectively

Society today teaches us that with great risk can come great reward. This can be true; however, the key differentiator is being mindful of what types of risks are worth taking.

In the world of business, the term "leverage" refers to the use of borrowed capital as a funding source to finance or grow operations; the goal ultimately being to amplify the rate of return on the money borrowed. A highly leveraged company is one that carries more debt than equity. Most startups rely on bank loans or investors to launch their businesses. Leveraging is an investment strategy, one that is always subject to some degree of risk. Indeed, not all ventures pan out: 20% of small businesses fail within the first year and only 50% survive the 5-year mark. Successful entrepreneurs must learn how to mitigate their level of risk as much as possible, while accepting the unknowns and moving forward with a tactical plan.

The second most common reason a business fails is the inability to secure enough capital to operate. While leverage is a fundamental aspect of business, it can easily feel like a heavy weight on the shoulders of a budding entrepreneur. Debt--it's that four letter word that strikes fear in the heart of millions of Americans. We naturally dislike owing something to others, yet most of us need to borrow for big purchases, such as a home or car.

Is this overwhelming fear of debt justifiable? As far as entrepreneurship goes, the reality is that most small businesses would be unable to grow without incurring some form of debt. Is there really a distinction between good debt and bad debt? Surely there are poorly judged investments; however, part of the issue is in framing, or reframing, how we perceive debt. Many see it simply as owing money to someone else (your financial liability) regardless of how it compares to what you own (your assets), leaving us with a skewed or incomplete concept of true debt.

Debt can be beneficial, if not essential, to business productivity and prosperity. The key is not to simply maintain more assets than liabilities, but to make smart purchase choices after thorough research and consideration and, perhaps most importantly, to seek the guidance of a knowledgeable financial professional.

Best Practice #5: Establish the Right Partnerships

Most successful entrepreneurs recognize the need to create professional partnerships and hire outside advisors to fill in the gaps of their business that require input on topics beyond their expertise. Global powerhouses like Starbucks and Facebook would struggle to survive today's business landscape without the guidance of skilled professionals who understand accounting, finance, strategy, and cash flow management. While there are several critical roles to fill when starting a business, finding an experienced financial professional team can literally make or break a company's viability. Many firms turn to certified public accountants (CPAs), management consulting firms, and wealth planning firms for an outside perspective.

When most people think of a CPA, they think of tax preparation. While this is a commonly sought out service, the scope of a CPA's skill set and knowledge extend far beyond taxes. Today, there are a range of specializations that a CPA may choose to work in, including forensic accounting and strategic business planning using financial statements and forecasting. From streamlining accounting processes to identifying financial weak spots, from budgeting and forecasting for healthy growth to implementing proper internal controls, strategic CPAs work with entrepreneurs to help them save money through improved efficiency and make their businesses more profitable.

Partnering with a CPA firm can also help business owners avoid the pitfalls of tunnel vision when difficult financial decisions need to be made. In fact, according to a study conducted by Intuit, creator of the popular accounting software QuickBooks, 89% of small businesses reported more success after hiring an accountant or other financial advisor to join their team.

It is also important to avoid the "one size fits all" approach when searching for a CPA. Finding the right partnership takes time and careful consideration. You should plan to meet with at least a few different prospective financial professionals. Ask questions to learn what they can offer and what they specialize in, check their credentials, and talk to references before making a final decision. You want to find a skilled professional with a proven track record who understands the needs of your business and is invested in your success. In addition to achieving proper tax preparation and compliance, a CPA can help identify key performance indicators that will impact your firm's financial statements and growth.

In Summary

Successfully scaling a business is a complex journey that not only requires sufficient cash flow, but also strategic thinking, insight, management skills, and adaptability. Sustainable growth is a balancing act of maintaining the right advisory teams, leadership personnel, and staff while distributing resources accordingly as the company builds. Unfortunately, many new entrepreneurs lack the appropriate knowledge and end up getting ahead of themselves, trying to run before they can walk. In fact, a leading cause of startup failure is premature scaling or attempting to do too much too soon.

Every business owner can use the support of a well-rounded and skillful team behind them. At Neumeister & Associates, our team of CPAs and staff are eager to help entrepreneurs take proactive control of their business strategy, operations, and finances, so that they can make carefully calculated decisions about the future. If you're ready to start the conversation, we invite you to reach out and connect with us today.

CHAPTER 7

HOW TO GROW YOUR ECOMMERCE BUSINESS

By **JENNIFER DIMOTTA**

It's no secret that eCommerce has dramatically transformed (and continues to transform) the world . In 2018, eCommerce celebrated a record-breaking year with global sales revenue estimated at $2.8 trillion. Plainly stated, if eCommerce were a country it would be number five on the world's GDP list.

Those numbers will only continue to rise. Consumers have grown accustomed to buying goods with the touch of a few buttons from the convenience of their couch. With eCommerce accounting for just 12 percent of the total retail sales around the world, the eCommerce market has extraordinary room for growth.

Online, eCommerce digital are all ways of selling products and services over a computer. It has transformed the way we buy and sell. Digital sales involves both imaginative experimentation and rigorous data collection. On one side, there is an opportunity to experiment and think outside the box, but on the other side there is data that can prove if such experimentation is effective or not. eCommerce has opened the opportunity to see what the consumer is doing along each and every step of the buying process. To be smart in eCommerce, marketers need to leverage that data. Be innovative and experiment, but remember that the more innovative you are, the more structured and disciplined you need to be to understand what the data is saying.

I started my career in the mid-1990s. At the time, no one had heard of online sales, digital marketing or eCommerce because it did not exist. Managing digital sales for big retailers like Sports Authority, Hayneedle, and Office Depot forced me to make up the rules as I went along. I had to create systems and methodologies for a way of selling that had no real history. Each time I started a new job I reflected on what techniques worked in my previous job and what techniques I could improve upon to create the ultimate methods for growing businesses online at an aggressive pace.

A few years ago I noticed the huge disparity in eCommerce sales between corporate giants like Amazon and Walmart and everyone else. To help mend this gap I started DiMotta Consulting in 2018. Using my 20 years of digital marketing experience I educate my clients about the world of online sales. Once they understand the opportunities in the digital landscape, they can begin aggressively growing their businesses.

In just two years, I grew Sports Authority from a $50 million company to a $225 million company. I believe in aggressive growth, but it is difficult to be both profitable and sustainable in the midst of this type of growth. For that reason, I created the DiMotta Method to help my clients grow aggressively with a profitable and sustainable methodology.

The DiMotta Method is for any industry, any size of business, and any level of eCommerce. It's a framework that creates organization and function in the Wild Wild West of eCommerce retail. Companies new to eCommerce are overwhelmed because this new way of selling can be very expensive, expert talent is limited, and the seemingly endless number of options makes prioritizing overwhelming.

The guiding principle behind the DiMotta Method is simple: aggressive, sustainable growth is possible with the right tools. My strategy is divided into four key steps: purpose, people, plan, and profit.

Purpose

It is essential to zero in on a business's goals and objectives before diving into the world of eCommerce. The clearer the purpose, the better. Grab a pen and paper. Write down and answer the following questions.

- What do you want to achieve?
- Are you looking to boost revenue?
- Do you want to supplement sales made in a brick-and-mortar or do you want to transition fully into a digital retailer?
- What do you want your annual sales to be in a year? Five years?
- What will be your market share in this time frame?

Once a company's purpose is established, it is easier to do a deep dive into that company's profits and performance to reveal the company's strengths, weaknesses, and areas for improvement.

People

People are the most important component to any business. They will either help drive success or they won't. Because they are at the heart of the business, they are also at the heart of the DiMotta

Method. Clear goals, detailed steps, and a strong infrastructure mean nothing unless an organization's staff knows how to implement them. Empowered, knowledgeable team members are vital to a company's success.

Even as eCommerce is having its day in the sun, many companies still do not have employees with sufficient digital knowledge. Leadership teams need training that goes beyond "Here is how to use social media." From my work in executive development, I know how important it is to help executives understand what it means to change the entire organization to start supporting a digital effort.

Digital has driven drastic mental model changes. The problems that businesses face aren't usually rooted in logistics–they're psychological. Many executive leaders, especially those who are employed at older, well-established companies, don't realize just how much value eCommerce provides. The risks seem too high and the transition feels daunting. This is when a shift in perspective is needed.

The speed at which wholesale or brick-and-mortar work is completed is much slower than eCommerce. The high pace of digital can be uncomfortable for the executives who are not used to that speed. Instead of taking eight to ten months to progress through, things are going to take eight to ten weeks or shorter to progress through. The type of speed can be scary to executives.

I work closely with executives to dismantle the mental models that hold their businesses back. I show leaders not only how much eCommerce can do for their company, but how quickly it can do it. I help executives analyze the data that digital provides to help them push back the fear. The advantages of the high speed of digital is that marketers can immediately see what is working and what is not. The more aggressive a business wants to grow, the more structure that is needed. My advice for companies who want to grow aggressively, but are just getting started in digital, is to put an expert in charge.

Plan

Once a purpose is established and the executives are inspired, it's time to take action. Shifting to eCommerce is never risk-free. With a plan that includes clear guidelines, however, the process will be as painless as possible.

The year-long plan is broken down by quarters and by months showing Owners, Tactics, Key Performance Indicators (KPIs), and Timelines. It is fully connected to the Purpose, which includes a Vision Statement and two to three Strategic Pillars. Each Tactic on the Plan connects to the Strategic Pillar and those share a KPI.

For example, when I was at Sports Authority, connecting to customers anywhere they wanted to connect was one of our Strategic Pillars in our Purpose. The Tactic was to have omnichannel capabilities so that customers could buy products online, pick them up in store, have them shipped from store, and check store inventory availability on the website. Timelines to accomplish each aspect of the Tactic were set.

The more aggressive the growth, the more detailed a plan needs to be. I work with companies to create a step-by-step process that eliminates the guesswork.

Profit

A profit and loss statement (P&L) is the guide that will get a business from where it is to where it wants to be. The P&L governs how a business will conduct itself. Every action that a company takes must be questioned as to whether it will affect the P&L positively or not. Any action that erodes profitability warrants a conversation as to whether it should be continued.

A P&L must be built from a bottom up perspective. P&Ls built from the bottom up often take one of several approaches. Some of them are built from how the business has performed by category and by marketing channel. It is easy to identify a growth trend to stick with by looking at recent growth rates.

In addition to historical trending, a P&L can identify opportunities for growth based on overall macro opportunity in a category or in a marketing channel. It can also identify areas to leverage more resources, like time, money and people within the company, to help position the company for growth. Having marketing provide a bottom up by marketing channel, merchandising providing a bottom up by product category can be very informative for the head of eCommerce to build out a final P&L plan also using the roadmap.

In addition, building out a bottom up from marketing and merchandising will inform marketing expense changes and gross margin adjustments, given that most businesses sell a variety of categories. When the mix of revenue changes, the gross margin often changes as well. A bottom up by category will give you the right insight into the right gross margin.

More often than not, I do not see the P&L built from the bottom up. That is one of the tactics I use to make sure I am profitably growing businesses in those triple digit zones on the revenue side.

When scaling business, it's important to keep an eye on all available data. Speed is key. It's critical to take a look at the P&L 30 days after the plan has been implemented. The results of this first month will establish a baseline and provide valuable insight into the company's trajectory.

Profit is important because it shows that the company is sustainable and has intelligent ways to grow revenue. For example, if a company is testing several promotions and spending a lot of money on marketing that cannot be tied back to the P&L, then there is a high chance the company will come out negative that month. Connecting those dots is extremely important if a company wants to grow profitably.

Frequent, thorough analysis of a P&L is the easiest way to figure out what's working and what isn't. Don't cling to a plan that isn't providing the desired results. The digital market world is always changing, and companies must adapt to maintain steady growth. Building a successful online business requires constant vigilance, but the P&L should be the ultimate decision-making tool.

The DiMotta Method was carefully crafted during my 20 years of participating in the growth of the digital marketplace. By focusing on the "Four P's" – purpose, people, plan and profit – marketing professionals and small business owners can reach their full eCommerce potential.

CHAPTER 8

RUNWAY LEADERSHIP

By **KATE YOAK**

My phone rang. It was Krish, the CEO I'd been advising from afar.

"Kate, I don't know what to do," he said. "I have been asking for project status and all I get is incomplete product demos. I spent eighteen months and two million dollars, and I have nothing to show for it. I am ready to fire everyone!"

Tech projects turnarounds are my specialty and I agreed to help.

What followed was a tragic discovery of how everything had gone wrong. The tech team said that they had a moving target. The chief technology officer felt, he had delivered on every request he had received from Krish. Meanwhile, Krish insisted, he had gotten nothing but brush-offs from his team and was casting blame on everyone from his executives to the most junior developer trying to type as fast as he could.

That summer I delivered the first incarnation of the Runway Leadership workshop to get Krish and his team back on their feet. It contained simple day-to-day advice on getting through the messy business of real-life leadership. It isn't about having formal authority or managing people. It is a toolbox for selecting action every single day as we execute on the runway, the grind, the place where the rubber meets the road.

A runway leader needs:

- Vision, visceral and dynamic, which enables him to know what to do and when
- Value-oriented communication to inspire others, empowering them to make the leader's vision their own
- Problem-solving approach for obstacles that get in the way
- Resiliency to bounce back from failure with positive momentum and no baggage

1. Visionary leadership

"No battle plan survives first contact with the enemy," nineteenth-century military strategist Helmut von Moltke once wrote. Indeed, no project plan prepares us for what's to come. To lead an army, a project, or a company, we must have a dynamic plan that we develop in our minds, but feel in our gut, in our fingers and toes. Our execution must be as natural as walking, scanning for obstacles, and picking a new path effortlessly through a visceral understanding of our goals.

First, to experience what I mean, I want you to think back to your childhood home (or one of them, the one that first comes to mind). It contains your memories, your experiences, the people that were around you. Your memory is clear – you can mentally walk room to room, each of which holds its treasures in your memory. And yet your recollection is full of blanks hidden away by time. You can live there in your mind, yet you don't recall every detail of your life. Set your reading aside for a couple of minutes and get that mental picture.

We are now ready to apply this concept to your next idea or project, fleshing it out until it's as visceral as that childhood memory.

Step 1. The idea.

Please select an idea for a business - the one you would work on if time and resources permitted. If no project is at the top of your mind, search for something that sounds interesting and worthwhile. Wait until you've got it.

Step 2. The future.

News flash: you did it! You built a company. It is successful beyond your wildest dreams. Since I don't know what those dreams are, I'd like you to answer the following questions about this future:

- What is the basic concept of your idea?
- There have been news articles about your success. Which publications?
- A celebrity has become taken with what you did. Who is that celebrity?
- How long did it take for you to make it happen?
- Did you hire a team? If so, what types of professionals did it consist of?
- Did your friends and family help? Which ones? What did they do?
- Did you keep your day job or plunge into it full-time?
- What is your role now? Are you running the company? Did you exit the business? Did you hire somebody to run it while you kept an advisory role?
- Who is your best client?

Spend some time adding to this image. Jot down any details that pop into mind. Visualize all of it in your mind's eye.

Note that visualizing success itself is superficial. While it's fun to see yourself in a limo with millions of dollars or being retired and spending time travelling, it's not what we are after. We are creating the childhood house version of the journey itself. It is so real, you could almost live in it, yet missing some details.

Step 3. Integrate your world.

Think of your life today. People you talk to. Things you are doing. How can those things add to the journey you are mentally engaged in?

Planning to visit family... isn't your cousin a photographer? You should talk to him and see if he has insights into image processing for your project...

The company where you work has started exploring chat bots. Getting engaged with that team might yield the much-needed expertise you are lacking...

You are already going to the trade show, perhaps you can look for cofounders with expertise in the space...

Keep going. Think of how every little thing you are already pursuing, every person you are already talking to, might add something.

Step 4. The real journey.

Of course, the journey you have just mentally created is still ahead of you.

We all process at different speeds. Over the next several days, look out for opportunities that jump out to you. You will notice that there are more people who can help or are excited about what you do than there were last week. News articles will suddenly pop out to you and contribute to what you have just mapped out in your mind's eye. Like a jigsaw puzzle, pieces suddenly snap into place.

If you pay close attention, it becomes a driving vision and, as it morphs and changes, you become the person who knows what to do and is ready for opportunity; challenges, once identified, become ready to solve themselves.

Your mental image has now been integrated into your intuition, resulting in a gut feeling when the project goes off track. You will intuitively know what to ask of your partners and subordinates until each piece snaps into a dynamic picture. Opportunities seem to come from thin air. The next step becomes intuitive and you will spot problems in your peripheral vision. But we are getting ahead of ourselves. We'll be talking about problem solving soon. First, we need to make sure our partners, subordinates, clients, and investors are on board.

2. Value-oriented communication

You just created a very personal vision, as intimate as your childhood memories. Over the next few days or weeks, you may find that you are triggered into action, filled with desire to make it come true and the energy to do what it takes.

Leadership communication is about doing this to the people you're working with. A great leader's vision is contagious.

We will now go back to the vision exercise and tailor it to the person you wish to inspire. To prepare, we need to find out a few things about this other person. What inspires and drives them? What are their dreams?

Their vision will, of course, be different from yours. Your job as a leader is to help build one around their values, not your own. They don't have your childhood memories; what's intimate to them is different.

Avoid the pitfalls of generalizing based on profession. Consider, for instance, what motivates programmers. Most of us assume it's something hard and mathematical. But when I ask this question in a workshop with programmers present, I am still astonished by the breadth of answers I receive.

Me: What's the most important aspect of your programming job?

Matt: "Working with people smarter than me."

Thomas: "Having a large variety of activities I can engage with daily. I never want to work with just one type of technology or have a repetitive routine."

Ben: "Improving the lives of coworkers I like. I want to come to work and expect I will make somebody's day better."

Kate: "Creating a conceptual mapping of the business process, which is necessary to create technology"

You see, programmers are as different as, well, people! So are salespeople, CEOs, designers, and project managers.

Here are some generic questions that will help you begin to understand what's special about this person, what makes them tick:

- What is most important to you in a job?
- If you had all the time in the world, what would you do with it?
- What professional position do you imagine holding when you retire?

Now go back to your mental image and see this person working with you. She is completely happy and dreams of making it come together. What is it like? Is she surrounded by people or working alone? Is she travelling around the world to pitch your idea or working from home into the night?

Ask her specific questions until you see the picture with her at the center. Then take the highlights of that picture and lay them out for her. When her eyes light up, you know you nailed it. If they never do, maybe it's the wrong fit. Move along and look for that light.

3. Problem-solving once and for all.

You have developed a vision that guides you through the hills and valleys, around immovable mountains and pitfalls. You spot obstacles just in time. Now we are ready to talk about what to do with the problems those obstacles represent.

Step 1. What is the problem?

"The problem is, my employees are not taking initiative," said a Polish tech company CEO in one of my workshops.

What he described was his unhappiness with the situation, not an obstacle that's in the way of accomplishing a specific goal. The statement pertains to his emotions more than anything else. So, his actions are likely to be emotional as well.

This is the biggest pitfall for most of us. We are consumed with our perception that the world is in the way of us achieving our goals. Unmotivated employees, the poor state of our culture, difficult economic conditions. Easy to latch onto, these are at best excuses for our failures.

Consider the following definition of a problem:
A problem is an obstacle that blocks a desired outcome.

This means that in order to identify the problem, you must first state the outcome you are after and then state your perceived obstacle. Finally, check whether this obstacle is truly blocking the path. Don't take a sledgehammer to a wall, but note if there is a door that leads in the right direction.

My workshop session with the Polish CEO proceeded down this path. We learned that his desired outcome was a well-functioning office network with good connectivity and printing services and that his employees prioritized other parts of their job, so things never happened. They weren't lazy or unmotivated at all; they just did not get his vision. From there, solutions were obvious: target date, requested deliverables, explicit priorities.

Step 2. Solve the problem.

That's where we roll up our sleeves and do the work. There is only one alternative: make the problem somebody else's.

A London-based CEO of an online apparel company was frustrated that developers and designers didn't stay in communication, so every detail required her attention. Together we designed a process that involved steps that forced the teams to interact for reviews and handoffs. Chasing the person down the chain became somebody else's problem. The successes and failures of the new process were evident from the progress shown on the company Trello board.

Step 3. Close the loop.

Did the problem get solved? Is the stakeholder happy? Did the Polish CEO get his office network? Is the process being followed in the London apparel company?

Have you noticed how often we jump to step two, provide a beautiful solution that does not actually solve the problem, and don't find out that the problem still exists months later? Skipping steps one and three, identifying the problem and closing the loop is like receiving a grilled cheese sandwich that's missing the slices of bread.

4. Resiliency with positive energy

You only get to succeed once: at the very end of your journey. Any other success is temporary, the final outcome unknown. Failure, on the other hand, is something you'll get to practice often on the way. Doing it well is critical, lest your journey end prematurely.

Typically, people have two ways they respond to failure: blaming themselves and blaming others. Most of us do both, yet tend to lean more one way or the other. Our goal here is to do away with both kinds of blame and replace them with the positive energy that comes from identifying the next step forward.

On Blame

Blaming others is obviously ineffective as we cannot fix them. In the problem-solving section, I described two CEOs, however well-intentioned, blaming others in place of identifying and solving problems.

The simply stated solution is: don't blame others. Find the problem and solve it. It's not that problem-solving is easy, it's that it is within our control.

On Guilt

This brings me to my favorite pastime: beating myself up. Take away blame and being inside my head gets mighty uncomfortable. If you are anything like that and calling yourself names is on your regular to-do list, I have a recipe that might just work.

Look in the mirror and realize that you are responsible for motivating the person you are staring at.

In other words, stop yelling at your best, most loyal employee who is your only hope for getting the job done. What do you do instead? Hopefully, you've been paying attention and have predicted my answer: identify the problem and solve it.

Remember Krish? Most of us have been in his shoes. If I have done my job, you can help him rescue his company. Develop a vision so real that you can tell the project is off-track and you are not getting what you need. Inspire the team, starting with your CTO, making sure that your vision is real and intimate to him, integrated around his own values. Note problems you need to get through to reach the finish line. And remember, failures and setbacks will happen. So, quit with the tantrums. If you are on the right track, you will see the light in the eyes of everyone who works for you. Your problems will become their own.

This is just the start of your journey. Practice visualization often and send me an email kate@runwayleadership.com with your experience. This is so important, I will personally respond to every message and help you get the most out of this toolbox!

CHAPTER 9

PURSUING YOUR DREAMS IS A LIFESTYLE

By **LAURALIE LEVY**

Lights are on in the youth hostel. I'm on a top bunk and three loud, drunk European men just fell into the shared bedroom. They're floundering around, speaking French and Dutch, trying to find unoccupied beds. I wake up but stay put. This is my first night living in New York City.

I first visited the city in my senior year of high school. It was April 2001, months before the World Trade Center fell. When I got to college, I framed postcards of different New York City sights and hung them up in my apartment. This from a girl whose home means Nevada. I had lived my whole life in the wide-open spaces of the West. Born and raised in Las Vegas. My mother was a wedding cake decorator and my father was a jewelry salesman in a pawn shop on the Las Vegas Strip. I moved to Reno, in northern Nevada, for college.

After graduation, I was one of the lucky ones. I had a job waiting for me back in Vegas and I took it. But that wasn't the goal. That wasn't what I wanted. I wanted New York. I was the Nevada girl with the big city dreams after all.

"I have news," I told my boss. "I am resigning. I am going to move to New York City."

"Do it!" she replied without batting an eye.

"Do it before you're knocked up and can't do it anymore!" she said fiercely from behind her desk, seven months pregnant.

So, there I was, wide awake in a youth hostel with my life packed in two suitcases. The dream had manifested; I was officially living in New York City. My ambitions were to get the best job and best apartment in the city in plus/minus two weeks.

What the hell was I thinking, though, really? Reality started to set in as I realized there were only so many days one could last in a youth hostel with five other people in one room. Those other people staggering around in the middle of the night. At that moment, I cried. What else can you do when faced with challenging truths? What had I done, how long could I last, why did I leave it all? So I could cry across the country in the middle of the night?

No, one moment does not a dream make. Even young and scared, the next morning brought new resolve. I'm here to accomplish a goal, I reminded myself. I'm here to face all the challenges and be on my own and have this experience. Why? Because I want it.

Because pursuing dreams is a lifestyle.

The first night in the youth hostel led to the first day in NYC. I roamed around the neighborhood, ate pasta at a restaurant, sat in the window alone watching the rain. I called family. I recruited help and formulated plans.

The second night in NYC was at a great aunt's house in Long Island, snuggled nicely in a warm bed.

Meetings with recruiters didn't bode well.

"How much money do you want to make?" the recruiter asked as I sat there, not a year out of college.

"At least $35,000," I said firmly. She stood up with a look of shock. That was too much money to ask for from such a fresh candidate.

"Let me show you out," she said as she escorted me to the door, her hand on my lower back

Another recruiter: "You'll need to dumb down your resume, so you don't appear overqualified."

Since when was that a problem fresh out of college?

Every day, I was at the computer searching for jobs, applying, writing cover letters, uploading my resume to job sites. I reached out to contacts of contacts. I had one mission: land the job! Each small step would get me inches closer to the end goal of being a part of the city in a way I wanted.

It would take six months of couch surfing with family and countless train rides into the city to actually "make" it into the city.

Then, there it was, a shiny office in City Hall Park and a big title. A prerequisite for working for city government was living in the city. The perfect storm, exactly what I had wanted. My office window looked out to the Brooklyn Bridge and I had the privilege of working in Downtown New York only one-and-a-half years after college graduation. All the way from the West Coast, this ambitious girl out of Vegas landed a job with the City of New York.

Then what? What happens when those small goals lead to accomplishing big dreams? What happens three years later? What do you do when your dreams start to change?

The thing about dreams is that they evolve. That's why it's less about the dreams and more about the lifestyle of living them.

My NYC dream felt like a chapter I got to live. And at some point, I felt that I needed a new one. The elected official I worked for was term limited; I felt like my time in the city was too.

"New York, I will see you later," I told that big city.

I moved back home to Las Vegas. Now, I had a reason to be there. I could start something. It felt like a place with familiar people, familiar streets, even a familiar home. I knew that I could make a few calls and the contacts I had there were all still around planting their roots in the city. I had left, I felt changed, but the purple mountains majesty called me back there, this time, with a real purpose- start my own business.

That is a good notion, a grand idea for a twenty-something to have but there was a reality to the situation. I didn't know what I wanted to do, exactly and I didn't have a plan.

I had no money, I had no food, I lived in a bedroom in my father's house that was mid-renovation and didn't even have carpet. I had no car. I let go of everything I had in NYC to go home and pursue a new dream but I started all the way back at the bottom.

So, penniless and hungry, I did what I had to do. I hustled. I got a part time job as a Monster Energy girl, just to be able to buy groceries for the house and put gas in dad's car. Even though I had just come off a big title and fancy New York City job, I knew that I had to do something to keep me afloat while I figured out what this new chapter entailed. There was a dream here, so no holds barred, I would do whatever it took. That dream is why after three years in NYC with an office and a window and a title and a salary, I left.

Then I found my idea. A friend and I got together and on a whim, thought we would start an online magazine. One fast decision turned into work immediately. We wrote, we edited, we attended events, we hosted events, we built a brand online using social media. I spent every waking moment marketing the publications and, for a while, it worked for me. I was happy. I was zoned in. I was following my gut.

But, the problem was, the young, fast and hustler way of doing things wasn't bringing us an income. This "business" I started wasn't making money fast enough. In fact, we never stopped to figure out a business model. We were spinning our wheels. We broke a few thousand followers online, received earned media and PR. We were close to selling ads or selling hosting, being "influencers" before that was a thing, but time was running out. After about nine months it was time to put more time or more money into this thing to make it profitable, to attach an actual business model to this publication I was treating like "work" and not a "company."

"We need more time or more money" was my idea.

"No." my friend responded. She had nothing left. She couldn't work for free anymore. Neither could I, to be honest. We were at the breaking point or the tipping point. Our team of two couldn't survive together to get to a tipping point, so we broke and the whole thing fell apart almost as quickly as it had risen to online fame.

I had believed that there was a light at the end of the tunnel and if we held out long enough we'd find our dream.

Yet, we weren't there. We hadn't made it, and the effort wasn't there to continue. I couldn't continue. It was time to face failure.

When the publication ended, it felt personal. It took the wind out of me. I didn't know how to deal with this particular dream ending and I felt paralyzed.

Alongside the personal failure was played the pain of poverty. All this work, and now... nothing. No money and no success. The sacrifice hadn't yielded a sustainable life and the dream had not materialized. When it all hit, when it all came tumbling down, when lawsuits from unpaid debt came in-I collapsed. I struggled to crawl out of the hole for months. I burdened everyone around me. It was painful and lonely. Telling people to believe in me appeared moot. I had been on a path that led to seemingly nowhere and I couldn't pivot in a way that released the burden. I felt guilty, I felt ashamed. My confidence was at an all-time low. It was unpretty and the failure felt almost insurmountable.

In the collapsing of it all, I was sad. It's hard, no matter how positive of a person you are, to come off a failure elated.

I thought I needed to concede and "find a job." I applied for many. I went through interviews. I got offers. I was miserable. Which job should I settle for, I wondered? I still wanted entrepreneurship but now I didn't know what to do.

I worked at Nordstrom for four days. I don't even know why I got the job there. I didn't want to work there. I didn't want retail. I had high hopes and didn't want to argue with the ladies who had a passion for bra-fitting when I didn't care. I just didn't. Now I'm back in Vegas to do this? No, this is not how this story ends.

I burst out, I couldn't do it, I quit.

If poverty was here, the only thing I could do was fight for my new dream, the dream of entrepreneurship. I've been lonely and poor before in a youth hostel in New York. I can do the hard things, even in the face of dreams blowing up! I realized, there was more misery in not going after my dreams than there would be in going ahead and forging on. I could not risk completely losing myself.

I asked my dad for more time borrowing his car and staying in his house. He didn't really mind, even though I faced the guilt about it often.

Pursuing dreams is a lifestyle and I knew it.

I learned that I needed to fight for the dream. That there was no time to waste. That the time is always now.

Back to the drawing board. How could I take the knowledge and skills of the past few years and sell it?

Both in my first job at the Chamber of commerce to the ivory tower in NYC to promo modeling and starting a digital publication, I was valuable. I had a new depth of experience that led to a unique skillset that not many others had, even if they had been at a job for years.

I had learned brand building, political affairs, online media, writing, speaking and positioning. This is where I found my niche. To me, it started to look like overall marketing and so that's how I decided to package this new offering. I knew I had a specialty with online marketing since the fast rise of the digital publication taught me how to do it. Slowly, I drew out plans for what could be a new business. No rash decisions, no business partner/best friends. Just me, slowly testing the waters with a new idea.

My first client for my marketing services came before the company had a name. I traded one hour for $50. In that hour, I consulted the client on marketing. I sat with her, I showed her how to work on a website and strategies she could use to promote her photography. I left the meeting, went to FedEx, and made business cards with just my name, phone number, and simply the title "social media marketing" listed. I spread the word about my capabilities, my experience building a brand and working across markets, about the new social media platforms Twitter and Instagram. I used the lessons of the previous experiences to build a business based on a new skill set I had developed through my successes and failures.

When I scored my first big client, the Las Vegas mayoral campaign, I was still feeling these pangs of poverty but the opportunity was perfect for me. It was to manage the online brand for the political candidate. This, I had done. This, I could do. This, was uniquely valuable to my experience in a way that I knew I could compete! In fact, two campaigns sought my expertise at the time. I had a choice and was able to decide from the beginning who I would work with.

At the time I got the contract for the mayor's race, I had $1.86 in my bank account. This one deal would help lift me up, give me confidence and allow me a case study that would show me the new potential business model at hand. Not only did the candidate win, she's won her reelection campaigns both times!

See, the pursuit is the challenge and the reward. It's booking the one-way plane ticket. It's proving that you really want "it" and stopping at nothing to get it.

Dreams are nothing without relentless pursuit, without picking yourself up in times of loneliness and failure and heartache, without living the lifestyle of someone on a mission, someone with goals. It's not always pretty and there are plenty of failures that come, both big and small that will test who we are. But if it's a dream to accomplish then it should be pursued. Dreams become goals, become actions, become reality, become memories.

I've been running Crowd Siren Marketing for a decade now and counting. Sometimes I wonder what I'd be doing had I stayed in New York working in government affairs. I wonder what would have happened if the digital publication reached it's tipping point and maybe I'd have over one hundred thousand followers on social media. And then I look at the dream I'm living now, the one where I rose up out of failure, where I am able to hire smart people and maintain a work life balance. Where I get to work with some of the biggest names on the Las Vegas strip, where I get to work with national and international brands. And this is the dream I settled into.

What dreams lie ahead now? How do I pursue them next? With care and tact, with baby steps, and missteps I'm sure. Relentlessly pursuing the next big project, the next big idea, the growing of my family and my body of work, the PR on my next race. Daily, I write about them, I map out a course, I take action, even if it's looking at the ideas on Pinterest and journaling about the dreams.

In moments of both uncertainty and clarity, I remember that the pursuit of the dream is the living of it. That the rollercoaster ride of that lifestyle is the exciting part and that there is always more out there to go dream about in our own lives. You just have to be willing to buckle up, no matter what.

CHAPTER 10

MANAGE YOUR ENERGY

By **LISA THOMSON**, DC, CFMP, CME

"Our most fundamental need as a human being is to spend and recover energy."

-Jim Loehr and Tony Schwartz, The Power of Full Engagement: Managing Energy, Not Time, Is the Key to High Performance and Personal Renewal (2003)

Matt sits in the reception room at my office sweating while he waits to be called back for his appointment. While my office is in sunny Southern California, the reason for the beadlets of sweat slowly dripping down his forehead this morning are not due to the heat but to the amount of pain and discomfort he is in. Tania, my office manager, offers him some cold water in an attempt to provide him some relief. As I approach the reception room, I see him sitting in the chair leaning on the left armrest as much as he can to take the pressure off the right side of his body. I invite Matt to one of my treatment rooms and he takes a seat.

"Well," I say. "What happened?"

"I woke up this morning and was going about my normal morning routine," Matt tells me. "Everything was fine until I bent over to tie my shoes. My low back just locked up. It hurts to even breathe. Can you fix me, Doc?"

Matt has been a patient of mine for years and by this point I know him well. Matt is one of my all-star athlete patients. He played Division I baseball and originally came to me because he knew that I had helped a lot of baseball players. After a successful collegiate baseball career, he landed a job at a large financial company. Two years ago, he left that company and started his own financial business. He always had had great leadership and entrepreneurial skills and his new company experienced success fairly rapidly. Once baseball was over, his business became his new competition and he was good at it. All of his focus had turned to growing his new business. Things like taking care of his physical and mental health quickly became secondary. He had gained about 30 pounds since he started his company and it was obvious that his stress level was on a continuous incline.

After going through a series of orthopedic tests and movement assessments with Matt to try and determine the source of his pain, I ask him a few questions.

"How has your stress level been lately?"

"Through the roof," Matt says. "I recently had to fire an employee who I found out was messing up some contracts we had with VIP clients. On top of that, my girlfriend wants to get married and start a family. I don't even have time for myself anymore it seems, let alone a family. I can tell my stress is starting to impact my business, too. I just feel like there is never enough time to get everything done."

"OK," I say. "How much sleep have you been getting?"

"Terrible," Matt begins. "I've been exhausted from putting in long hours at work, but I can't seem to get a good night's sleep. On a good night, I get about 6 hours."

"OK," I say again and have a feeling I already know the answer to the next question, but I ask anyway.

"How has your diet been lately?"

"Also terrible," Matt says. "I just don't have the time to make myself healthy food. I have been eating out for most of my meals. I am at my desk almost all day and it's just easier to pick up food from one of the local fast food chains than it is to make a healthy lunch. And I know this isn't good, but I usually have a few beers at the end of the night because I think it helps me relax."

It is apparent that Matt's pain is not due to a specific injury; his pain is due to his lifestyle.

Unfortunately (or fortunately depending on how you look at it) your body will let you know when you are not taking proper care of it. To be successful in life, whether it is our personal life or our business career, taking proper care of yourself is nonnegotiable. The energy we have and the energy we give may be the most important determinant in our success. Let's break down four of the main contributors to Matt's current painful situation that are draining his energy.

Stress

That feeling when you're late for an important meeting: your heart rate increases, your breathing quickens, and beads of sweat begin to appear. This is what is known as the 'fight or flight' response. This is our sympathetic nervous system preparing our bodies for what is being perceived as a potential threat. If this happens when there really is a threat (being inside of a burning house, for example) the newly heightened senses are beneficial. The problems start happening when the fight or flight stress response is activated too frequently. Some problems associated with higher stress levels include cardiovascular disease, weight gain, diabetes, anxiety, depression, poor sleep, accelerated aging, and premature death. If stress levels are high for an extended period of time, damage is being done to your mind and body.

Fortunately, people have the ability to counter this stress response. If you don't have a good, healthy stress reliever, it is time to find one.

There are three tools that I recommend to my patients to combat the stress response.

1. **Some form of meditation, breathing, or calming technique.** It should be able to immediately combat the stress response. Studies show that meditation can help suppress the stress response and lower blood pressure, reduce anxiety, and decrease inflammation. Other breathing and calming techniques work great, as well. Try a few different methods, find one that works for you, and do it every day.
2. **Movement.** We will touch on this topic more when we talk about movement and exercise a little bit later in the chapter.
3. **Having a good support system and being unafraid to ask for help**. There are people who want to see you succeed and care about your wellbeing. Don't be afraid to reach out for help when it is needed.

Sleep

Sleep plays a vital role in our overall health and wellbeing. Sleep is our body's recovery time and it is essential to functioning at your highest potential. Studies show that adults need seven to nine hours of sleep per night. There are many reasons why people aren't getting enough sleep. I will touch on a few of the most common ones.

1. **Lack of movement throughout the day.** Exercise, as long as it is not right before bedtime, can help you expend some of your energy during the day, which often leads to better sleep.
2. **Alcohol.** It is a common misconception that alcohol helps you sleep better. While it may help you fall asleep, alcohol reduces the quality of sleep by shortening the amount of time spent in rapid eye movement (REM) sleep. Alcohol should not be used as a method to help you sleep better as it is most likely doing the opposite.
3. **Stress.** As discussed above, higher stress levels negatively impact sleep quality.
4. **Too much light.** Light sends a signal to the brain that it is time to be awake. This can be light from a lamp, the glow of an alarm clock, or the screen of your phone. Having screen time before bed in the form of cell phones, computers, TVs, etc., can have a seriously negative impact on your sleep.
5. **Hormones.** There are many hormonal factors that can come into play when it comes to sleep. If you think this might be the cause of your poor-quality sleep, contact your medical provider.

Movement

I intentionally used the word movement here instead of exercise. Movement and exercise are often thought of as hard work. While it is important to challenge yourself and make some exercises 'hard,' movement should not be thought of as extra work. Movement should be thought of as an essential part of being human.

Our bodies function optimally when moving. Moving affects our circulation, improves joint health, reduces stress, improves energy levels, and improves brain function. If you want your body to feel good as you age, keep moving.

Diet

We all know that a poor diet can have serious consequences for our health. When it comes to health and the energy that we have, changing your diet can be life-changing. A quick search on Amazon.com for diet books yielded over 70,000 results. Different things work for different people and we won't get too far into the details of what we should eat and why. There are a few guidelines, however, that are important to note when it comes to the food we eat.

1. **Avoid highly processed foods.** Processed foods are typically made for convenience rather than nutrition. These foods often have harmful additives and can wreak havoc on the body. Some examples of processed foods include frozen pizza, potato chips, and deli meats.
2. **Drink plenty of water.** There are many factors that come into play when trying to determine the amount of water that a person needs per day. To make things easier, I typically recommend going by the color of your urine. Poorly hydrated individuals usually have a dark yellow or orangish urine color. Hydrated people typically have a pale yellow or even colorless urine.
3. **Avoid sugar as much as possible.** Sugar intake has a strong connection to conditions such as obesity, heart disease, depression, diabetes, and cancer. Sugar is inflammatory, highly addictive, and can damage your brain, kidneys, liver, and heart. To maintain higher energy levels, sugar intake should be avoided like the plague.

4. **Avoid foods with ingredients that are difficult to pronounce.** These are typically chemical additives that can be harmful to the body.
5. **Eat real, unprocessed foods** that your grandmother would recognize as food.

So, what happened to Matt's back? Due to Matt's lifestyle, his body and brain were functioning at a less than optimal level. Bending down to tie his shoes didn't cause his back pain, lack of sleep, high stress, poor diet, and lack of movement did. Within a few visits, we were able to take care of his pain. We had a serious discussion about his daily habits and how they were affecting his health and energy.

About six months later, Matt came back to my office. This time, instead of grimacing in pain as he waited to be called back, he had a content grin on his face. In the treatment room, I asked him the same question I had asked him a few months prior.

"What happened?"

"The back pain I had six months ago opened my eyes to the choices I was making," he told me. "I got into some bad habits and it was impacting all aspects of my life. I set goals and made serious changes to how I was taking care of myself."

His newly restored sense of energy was contagious.

"I wanted to thank you, Doc. Since I last saw you, I hired a few new employees to help with the day-to-day operations at my office and to help take some of the load off my back. I made sleep and stress reduction top priorities. I've been eating better and exercising more, and I cannot believe how good I feel."

The person that was speaking was a seemingly different person than the one that came to me in pain.

"What I didn't expect was how taking better care of myself made such a huge impact on my personal and professional life. My business just had the best week financially to date and I am happy to say I just got engaged."

Matt's story is one that is far too common. We need to make our health a top priority.

Maintaining your energy is the key to success.

CHAPTER 11

THE INGREDIENTS OF EMOTIONAL MARKETING

By **MARCO BALDOCCHI**

Who among us is not able to feel any emotion? No one.

This is the real reason why the new era of marketing is based on emotions more than ever before. Marketing is an ever-changing, adaptive industry and we must continue to find new ways to appeal to consumers.

Emotional Marketing is a marketing strategy that uses emotions as leverage to tear down the psychological resistances to buy. The emotions are a very powerful motivation because they bring the consumer into a memorable, engaging, all-encompassing story in which they are the main actor.

Did you know that 95% of your decisions are made following an emotion, using the center and middle parts of your brain (called the reptilian brain and the limbic brain) and just the remaining 5% are made using the outer, more rational part of your brain (called the neocortex)?

We examine information and make decisions through the cooperation of two systems: one emotional and the other rational or logical.

The emotional system is made up of our reptilian brain (the instinctual brain, the part that recognizes dangers, needs, and manages automatic behaviors like breathing) and limbic brain (the emotional or feeling brain, the part of our brain that produces dopamine and serotonin). Our emotions are automatic and subconscious; this part of your brain jerks quickly, is not always easily managed, and almost always determines purchasing decisions. The rational system is slower, more manageable, and it works at a conscious level, which allows us to think through and rationalize decisions we've made.

The emotions are always active, ready to move at all times, and are what tend to imprint indelible memories. Think of your clearest memories from your childhood. They are almost always connected to a strong emotion: joy, anger, fear.

The emotional marketing goal is to turn on these emotional triggers to let the consumer (user) live a fully immersive experience that catches their attention and lets them feel like the protagonist of an inalienable story.

In this way, an effective relationship is established between the brand and the customer, based on positive feelings and deep emotions, founded on respect and love. These are the right motivations that get the user to buy and, in the time, to build customer loyalty.

Remember, nowadays people don't choose a product for its features but for the emotions the product will let them feel while using it. Look at how Apple markets its products - as cool, must-have items that make you feel young, cool, hip, and on top of the trends.

The Ingredients of Emotional Marketing

At its core, Emotional Marketing listens to the consumers to understand them better, learns to anticipate their unconscious wants, and then repeats those wants back to them in ads, which stimulates their emotions and satisfies their wants.

Emotional Marketing utilizes storytelling to be able to make people relate to the ads and see themselves in them, by using exciting language and attractive and engaging images. These are the essential ingredients for a successful Emotional Marketing strategy.

Storytelling

Storytelling is a common communication technique that consists of telling a story using the typical narrative elements. In persuasive stories, there is always a protagonist (the main character) who has to overcome a problem, an antagonist who opposes the protagonist, and a helper or tool that offers support to the protagonist, and it all culminates in a happy ending.

The purpose of storytelling in Emotional Marketing is to help the potential client see themselves in the role of the protagonist and focuses on evoking strong emotions so as to induce him to act or make a purchase.

In Emotional Marketing, the helper or tool that comes to the rescue will be your brand, which solves the problem the protagonist faces or has to overcome. In the simplest of terms, you want to tell a story where your product or service is the solution to an everyday problem many people can identify with.

Language

Emotional Marketing speaks to the heart. You want the language and imagery used in your Emotional Marketing campaigns to involve all of the senses. You want the consumer to be able to feel, touch, hear, see, and even taste everything.

Think of the marketing campaigns from Apple, Coca-Cola, and Ikea. They are all national and international brands that put emotions, stories, and people and their daily experiences at the center of their campaigns. An Emotional Marketing campaign works by making people feel like they are a part of a small community in which users can recognize themselves and feel the same things.

Images

Whether it is graphics, photos, or videos, images play a fundamental role in the first interaction with potential consumers, so you must use an approach that is visual and immediately engaging.

Most people take less than three seconds to see something and formulate either a positive or negative response.

In Emotional Marketing, images have the important role of grabbing the attention of the consumer, capturing them emotionally, and convincing them to pause, look, read, discover, and go deeper.

Emotions & Needs That Trigger Purchasing Decisions

Now that you know emotions push us to decide, take action, and drive purchasing decisions, let's take a closer look at the emotional triggers (both positive and negative), needs, and desires that marketing strategies often try to tap into and focus on to encourage purchases.

Fear

Fear is a very powerful emotion. In marketing strategies, it can be exploited in two ways. One is by telling people how that product or service can help them solve the problem they fear, and the second is by leveraging the concept of scarcity and creating urgency, which taps into the fear of missing out on something.

Guilt

Guilt is another powerful, if negative, emotion. If you have an effective and concrete solution that is able to alleviate some sort of guilt your potential customer has, they will be grateful to you. For example, if the person is feeling guilty about gaining weight, your weight loss product or service can help them. Another example is anti-smoking ads making parents feel guilty for putting children at risk with second-hand smoke.

Trust

In order for people to convince themselves to buy something from you, they have to trust you. Trust and mistrust are both emotional processes, and a consumer trusting you is fundamental in every purchasing decision. How can you get people to trust you?

A few ways are by offering them advantageous return policies, giving away a free trial of your service, and concretely showing results they can achieve using your product or service.

In this context, trust can also come from positive reviews from those who have already had a shopping experience with you. Likewise, pay close attention to negative reviews, because they can trigger a dangerous word of mouth unfavorable to your reputation, but can also be useful to you by showing you specific ways you can improve your product, service, purchasing process, and other things. Negative feedback is something you, as a brand, can learn from. When a company responds to negative feedback and makes changes, it shows consumers that you listen to them, which also fosters trust.

The Need to Belong

Tribes have existed since mankind has existed. The sense of belonging to a community has always been fundamental, because it makes us feel accepted, less alone, and protected.

That is why today it is very important for brands to build a community (often using social media) within which their customers feel involved, important, heard, and safe. This taps into the essential human need for being heard and feeling a sense of belonging and community.

The Desire for Immediate Gratification

We are in the age of speed and immediacy. We do not like to waste time, and if there is something we want, we want it to have it immediately. Exploiting this desire for instant gratification can become a powerful driver to buy. One example is Amazon Prime and the ability to get anything you want in 24-48 hours. Remember when people used to wait two weeks for packages? Neither does anyone else. Immediacy has become the norm.

The Desire for Great Value

It is fundamental to make the potential client perceive that what they are buying has a very important value, or that taking advantage of your promotion is allowing them to get greater value for less money.

You can build your marketing campaigns by focusing on the value that your good or service will bring to the consumer. When using value as your unique selling proposition, you don't want to focus too much on the technical details, and instead focus specifically on the value your product brings to users.

The Desire to Be First

Many people make purchasing decisions based on wanting to be first, at the start of a trend, an early adopter of something new and exciting. This desire to be first and trendy can be a strong emotional desire. Take advantage of this desire by highlighting want makes your product or service new or unique, and use testimonials and popular social media influencers in your marketing campaigns. People often enjoy imagining themselves living the life of influencers they follow.

Strategic Experiential Modules

Your goal as a marketer must be to have your customers love what they bought from you. To that end, I want to introduce to you the concept of Strategic Experiential Modules. These are five categories of experiences that can be brought to life through your marketing strategies and campaigns which most consumers will relate to.

You don't want to just sell something to someone one time. You want to create trust and build loyalty. Experiential Marketing will help connect you with consumers in a new way. Here are five types of experiences you can bring to life with your brand.

1. The Sensory Experience

Marketing campaigns using sensory experiences focus on the involvement of one or more of the five senses, which are sight, hearing, touch, smell, and taste.

Smell is our most powerful sense and it can trigger memories and emotions, so one example may be to incorporate aromas into your product or packaging. One company that has done this recently in a very successful way is CoverGirl, who released both peach and chocolate-scented eyeshadow palettes, which have become popular. While this may be a novelty or gimmick, it boosted sales.

Taste is another sense you can incorporate, with events revolving around food or products or marketing campaigns tapping into nostalgic tastes and flavors. Hearing is easy to incorporate with music. Touch and sight can come into play with the packaging.

Sensory experiences are effective because they exert a strong influence on the consumer, who, once attracted to a color or smell, will have a pleasant impression of the product or service.

2. The Emotional Experience

We have been discussing the use of emotions in this chapter, and there are many ways to tap into smaller daily emotions and relatable experiences of your consumers.

From the scent of coffee in the morning to reading a favorite book during the commute to work to getting frustrated in rush-hour traffic, every day is composed of many "micro-experiences," repetitive or non-repetitive actions that fill our time and change our mood.

If a brand manages to connect these experiences with the consumers, it will create an indissoluble bond with them, and they will remember the brand and the experience or emotion every time he sees their logo, products, or services.

The Emotional Experience is widely used in "feel good" campaigns, those in which the goal of the brand is to get in tune with consumers and create good emotional experiences with which to "tie" the customer to their brand. One example is when brands show that they are socially conscious or that every purchase helps someone else in the world, such as Warby Parker, TOMS, and Out of Print Clothing.

3. The Intellectual Experience

To provide intellectual experiences in consumers, you are aiming to provoke, surprise, or intrigue them. These are often creative and cognitive experiences, which base the consumer's involvement in mental actions and, therefore, creates a strong bond because they are thinking and/or learning. This is an enduring tactic because it sticks with the consumers, which makes it effective.

The intellectual experience pushes consumers to interact with the brand and the product or service in a cognitive or creative way, so one example may be when we ask questions or challenge consumers by offering them new ways to solve old problems.

It is very important not to overdo this emotional marketing strategy because there is a risk of making mistakes and getting the opposite result is very high. Do you remember the incredible clamor caused by CarPisa case in 2017?

For one product launch, CarPisa decided to exploit this marketing technique in an original way, which ended up causing the opposite of what they wanted and embroiled them in controversy.

CarPisa's campaign was that once a purse was purchased, the customer was invited to draw up a marketing and communication plan and send it to them. Whoever created the best plan would win a 30-day unpaid internship at the company!

They were absolutely slaughtered by the community of communication specialists, who accused them of exploitation and just wanting free work from professionals; they had the point that CarPisa was asking them to purchase their product then do hours of free work, only to "win" a prize of a whole month of more free work.

So, my advice is to know and understand your audience and study their needs and reactions very well before using this type of strategy. This is certainly a functional strategy, but can be incredibly dangerous if it backfires. You want to stimulate and amaze your customers, but it is very important to remember to analyze and anticipate their reactions as much as possible, otherwise, you risk losing clients and their trust.

4. The Action Experience

These are experiences that involve interacting with your consumers in person and leading them to perform physical or mental interactions with your product or services. This category of Emotional Marketing makes use of motivational, persuasive, and instinctive messages which serve to push the customer to act differently than how they would normally behave and to try new experiences that could change their life for the better.

Often this type of communication tries to help the consumer test their limits and encourages them to face and overcome them. This can include showing the person strongly persuasive images that represent the emotions that they are trying to overcome, showcase their limitations, and encourage them to break down their barriers and get out of their comfort zone.

One simple example is the way Nike ads always push consumers to go beyond their limits with "Just do it."

5. The Relational Experience

As the Greek philosopher, Aristotle wrote in his 4th-century work Politics, "Man is a social animal." It is, for this reason, we naturally tend to congregate with others and try to establish ourselves within society.

To understand how innate this behavior is, back in the Paleolithic era, when mankind was still nomadic, they already lived in groups, where the first goal of the group was survival.

Creating experiences that put the consumer in a relationship with a group of people similar to them, those who have similar aspirations and interests, is the foundation of relational experiences. By doing so, you are able to stimulate the individual's personal aspirations and ambitions and create a strong relationship within a group they belong to, which is in line with their idea of their "ideal selves."

Leveraging the desire for personal progress and elevation of one's status in a social context will lead consumers to see your product or service as the key to improving their lives and social position.

Conclusions about Emotional Marketing

Excite your consumers, but do it with honesty and transparency. This is the principle that drives Emotional Marketing, and what will make you win the affection, respect, and trust of people.

In one of my recent campaigns, I decided to use Augmented Reality technology to excite potential consumers of a brand that had hired me as a strategic planner. Why? Because I love mixing the real-world and the digital world to generate an exciting experience and tap into the emotions of people.

CHAPTER 12

HOW DO YOU DEFINE CONFIDENCE?

By **MARGUERITA CHENG**

In the financial services industry, there is a misconception that a confident person is loud, aggressive, and overbearing. Measured against that definition, I am not confident. If, however, confidence means someone who listens first to understand, someone who collaborates with clients, someone who believes in themselves when others may doubt them, someone who finds resilience deep within themselves, then I am confident.

For me, the simplest definition of confidence is believing in yourself when others doubt you. Of course, competence is essential to workplace success. But competence will only take you so far without confidence. If you do not believe in yourself, how can you expect anybody else to believe in your skills and abilities?

In my journey as a successful entrepreneur and financial advisor, I have come to realize that confidence has been a key component to my 20-year career. It helped me develop my own style of sales when I first started as a financial planner, it helped me connect with my clients, and it eventually led me to start my own investment advisory firm, Blue Ocean Global Wealth.

My first confidence test came two years into my career as a financial advisor at a large financial services firm. When I started that position, I had technical knowledge, but lacked sales experience. I also did not have a large network of friends and family who could be potential clients. Starting from this point, I did exactly what my sales manager told me to do. He advised me to start making cold calls and that is exactly what I did. My first year I had 33 clients and 31 of them were from cold calls. It turned out to be great advice, but after two years of that I hit a wall. I think I was exhausted. I never gave myself a chance to just come up for air.

I struggled with sales. I did not want to be perceived as pushy. I felt that many of the "successful" advisors talked down to clients or talked over their clients' heads. Instead of following this example, I took my time listening and understanding my clients' goals & dreams. I also wanted to know their fears & concerns so I could serve them best. My thought process was that in order for people to do business with you they have to like you and they have to trust you. When people connect with you, they feel comfortable with you. You can't ask people to buy in if you do not offer them the chance to weigh in.

After a while, I realized that my approach resonated with others. People do business with those they like and trust. My superpower was my ability to relate and connect with others. My manager said to me, "Rita, you are very technically sharp, but you are a lousy financial advisor. You spend too much time listening, asking questions, and relationship building." He led me to believe that being empathetic and patient was a liability.

I was a young employee with just a few years of experience in the field. When he said this to me, I hit the pause button to think about what he was saying. From his vantage point, he was right: I was a horrible financial advisor because I did not push enough for the sale. But I wanted to prove that I could be successful serving my clients in another way. My way might not work with the people he wanted to work with. I knew that. But the way I connected with people was truly meaningful for them and I was not taking anything away from anybody.

I had to tap into my inner confidence to admit that he was right for what he wanted to do, but that his style did not serve me because it did not attract the clients I wanted to serve or the experiences I wanted to deliver. I wasn't arrogant, but I was confident. I knew that what I was doing was innovative.

At that point, I felt confident enough to tell my manager that for me to get to the next level I needed to make this mine. I believe in learning from your mentors, but at some point along the way you begin to develop your own style and you need to have confidence to break from the norm and do things your own way. My vision was bigger than my boss's vision. I didn't want to just sell stuff, I wanted to impact the industry. I wanted to change the world and I knew I was not going to be able to do big things if I did things like everybody else.

Self-doubt did pop up in those early years of following my own path, but my clients kept me going. They said, "It is different with you, Rita. I have never felt this comfortable with anyone else." That third-party validation from the clients I served let me know that I was on the right track. Confidence is not just about doing things your own way no matter what; it is always important to check in with the people you are serving to make sure your style is fitting their needs.

Since then, I have built my career as a financial advisor, consultant, speaker, and writer on my own terms. I promise that attaining a deep sense of self-confidence will propel you to the next level, give you the strength to stay true to your values, muster through self-doubt, and overcome setbacks. Here are six ways to boost your confidence.

1. Define what success is to you

Early in my career I studied my peers who were deemed "successful" by outside standards. I noticed that they had a habit of talking down to their clients and using aggressive sales tactics. I found that troublesome. I felt that that approach gave the financial industry as a whole a bad rap. I knew immediately that was not the type of success I wanted. Instead I wanted to connect with my clients and get familiar with their needs. I wanted to be a good representative of myself, my firm, and the financial services industry.

That way of success was not right for me, it was not right for the type of success I wanted to deliver, so I began developing a more personal style of sales that was aligned with my version of success.

My definition was not the standard definition that involves quickly closing sales. I defined success by implication ratio, by how many people actually implemented my advice and by the number of referrals I was getting. I had a high client retention and satisfaction. Knowing this and hearing great client feedback lead me to start gaining self-confidence and doubting myself less. The third-party validation helped me realize that I could be successful doing things my own way.

It is important to remind yourself that everyone has a different definition of success. I knew I was different from my co-workers, so wouldn't it make sense that my values and priorities were different?

How do you define success for yourself? What does success mean to you? For me, success is finding work that is intellectually stimulating, emotionally gratifying, and financially rewarding with positive societal impact.

2. Know your worth

Confidence is knowing you have something of value to bring to the table. Even if you are a young entrepreneur without much experience, you still have new perspectives and insights that are valuable. When I was new to my field, I did not know how to close a sale, but I was very good with technology. I could fix technical issues, I could teach people how to use their financial calculators, and I could review the inputs and outputs from the financial planning software, not to mention I was able to troubleshoot technology issues. With this knowledge I became indispensable in the office. Having something of value to offer builds trust and credibility with managers, coworkers, and clients. Figure out what it is that you bring to the table.

3. Let values drive your decisions

I left Ameriprise in part because I wanted to put my family before my career. At the time, my father was struggling with Parkinson's disease. I was not able to spend the amount of time with him that I wanted to while I was working for a large firm. When I cared for my dad, I could write articles and develop continuing education programs for Certified Financial Planner® professionals.

I knew I had to take a step back to move forward. I had to quit the job I had had for the past 14 years, the job that I had built my career on up until that point. But, at the end of the day, I knew that family was more important than a career, so I chose family. Once you put hard decisions into perspective like that, they become easier to make.

4. Be fearless

Having confidence means being fearless in the face of adversity. It is true that some of the most challenging experiences in our lives can be the best things that happen to us. It is not easy for us to understand while we are experiencing them, however. Be risk aware, not risk averse. Don't let risk hold you back, and don't take failure personally.

I struggled with the decision to leave Ameriprise to spend time with my father while he was sick. I asked myself why I would take a step backward. It took a lot of confidence to make that move. Of course, it was stressful, but I chose family. My dad has since passed away. As painful as it was to walk away from that position, I am so grateful that I made that decision to spend time with my dad before he died.

Just as Kathrine Switzer says, there is no age limit on fearlessness and inspiration. Switzer was the first woman to officially enter and complete the Boston Marathon. Her story inspires me to be Fearless in the face of adversity, whether it is preparing for a tough marathon or dealing with the challenges that life presents us.

5. Know your strengths

When I started my career, financial advice was undervalued. People would give it away if you bought a product from them. I wanted to do things differently. I wanted to deliver financial advice separate from asset management. I started listening to my clients' needs and connecting with them on a deeper level. At times, I was criticized for not being aggressive enough. My approach to sales was unconventional, but I attracted an underserved clientele that was turned off by the financial services industry. I focused on what I did best, which was connecting with people. For this, my clients appreciate me and my career continues to prosper.

6. Trust your intuition

In 2007, right before the global financial crisis, I noticed that a bond mutual fund had lost eight percent in one year. My intuition told me that something was wrong. I told my clients that I was nervous about this mutual fund. I did not have a concrete reason why, but I let them in on my hunch.

The next year that same fund lost more than 40 percent. People in my network ask what I did with that and I said I sold it a year ago. When they asked me why, I told them that the eight percent loss made me uncomfortable. I am not suggesting that I forecasted the market collapse, but trusting my intuition lead me to make smart financial decisions for my clients before the eventual crash. I felt confident telling clients, "If I am wrong about this you can deduct your tax loss for the year and we can purchase this next year. If I am right, you can keep your money in cash and write off the losses." I have always been able to communicate with people in an honest respectful manner. It takes confidence to be completely honest with your clients, but there is no better way to do business.

CHAPTER 13

THERE IS NO SIGHT LIKE FORESIGHT: FORESEE LEGAL PROBLEMS BEFORE THEY ARISE

By **PARAG AMIN**

As the principal of my own law firm that specializes in civil litigation, I have seen countless businesspeople enter into agreements and deals before thinking through the potential issues. Often, the business scales and unanticipated one or more disputes arise, and they hire my firm to litigate and resolve the dispute. Sometimes it is a dispute with a customer, other times it is a dispute between the co-owners of a business, and sometimes it is a dispute with a vendor. Nevertheless, one similarity between disputes is that many of the issues could have been prevented if the clients had anticipated some of the problems before they arose and considered solutions while the problems were only hypothetical.

Early in business, many entrepreneurs take a do-it-yourself approach to legal issues. They are used to "figuring things out" for themselves and sometimes there is a temptation to save money on legal advice. In that regard, business founders might download a contract template from the Internet and find and replace a few words or use an online legal service that gives them a boilerplate contract. That approach may be fine when the numbers are small, but as the business scales, the money an entrepreneur invests in wise legal advice will pay dividends because a dispute is almost always more expensive to resolve after it arises than if you anticipate and address it before it arises.

Even if a disagreement does not result in litigation, the dispute can cost your business time and energy that could and should have been invested in growing the business or improving customer experience. A simple example that arises frequently in most businesses is what happens if a contractor fails to timely complete a project or task. That contractor's failure to complete his, her, or its task on time can lead to consequential damages for the business and result in lost time and/or profit. That risk is best considered and allocated before the problem arises.

For example, I had a client who had an online retail business that used television ads to attract customers. After one of her television ads aired, thousands of people who saw the commercial visited her website to purchase products. However, the website was slow, and she decided to upgrade it to expedite order fulfillment. Unfortunately, the developer she hired failed to correctly optimize the backend code of the new website. So, the next time one of my client's commercials aired during an NFL playoff game, her website crashed, and my client lost hundreds of thousands of dollars in potential sales.

The site crashing meant that the backend developer was probably liable to my client for all of her lost sales. However, before we filed the suit, we had to consider whether the developer was financially capable of compensating my client for her losses. Another inevitable issue was that the developer blamed the hosting company for the site crashing, which, unsurprisingly, the hosting company denied.

Unfortunately, my client came to my firm after the agreement was entered and after the website had crashed. If she had hired my law firm before she entered the agreement with the website developer, we would have advised her to consider the chances of failure for the new website and would have required the developer to obtain insurance that compensated my client if the website failed to perform as promised for whatever reason. This would have resolved the issue of liability and the possible collectability issue regarding the developer's inability to pay for the potential losses. We would have also insisted that a few other key provisions be included in the agreement, such as a mediation provision, an arbitration provision, and a prevailing party attorney's fees provision.

The first provision you should consider including in your contracts is a mediation provision. A typical mediation provision requires each party to mediate any disputes between them prior to filing a suit. This provision is often helpful in resolving disputes before they escalate and go into full-scale litigation. Mediation is a form of alternative dispute resolution in which the parties hire an independent individual to help them resolve their dispute. Usually, the mediator is a lawyer or retired judge who has experience in the specific area of law involved. Mediating a disagreement can save parties time and money if they are able to resolve their dispute before filing a lawsuit.

The second provision you should strongly consider including in your agreements is an arbitration provision. Arbitration is a private alternative to the public court system. In arbitration, one or more arbitrators, depending on the type of arbitration selected, act as both the judge and jury in applying the law to the facts and reaching a decision. Arbitration is usually faster than litigating a case in state or federal court. Another benefit of arbitration over filing in court is that in both state and federal court you do not get to choose your judge based on that judge's experience, background, or interests. When you file a lawsuit in state or federal court, typically you are automatically assigned to a judge without regard for the judge's prior experience with that type of case. For example, if you have a breach of contract case involving a licensing deal, and you file a lawsuit in state or federal court, you are not necessarily going to get a judge who has any kind of interest or background in licensing agreements. You are playing litigation roulette and hoping that the randomly assigned judge for your case has a background, interest, or understanding regarding your type of dispute. On the other hand, with arbitration you can specifically choose an arbitrator based on their background, education, experience, and other factors. Although you will pay hourly for the arbitrator's time, the arbitration process can reduce months or possibly years in litigation time, which means you can often get the dispute resolved faster and go back to focusing on your business sooner.

A third provision that a you should strongly consider including in contracts is a prevailing party attorney's fees provision. Many people are unaware that in the United States the general rule is that the winner and the loser in a lawsuit are each responsible for paying their own attorney's fees. The only two exceptions to this rule are when there is a contractual provision or when there is a statute that allows the prevailing party to recover its attorney's fees. In a business versus business litigation dispute, most of the time there is no applicable statute that allows the winner to recover its attorney's fees. So, unless there is a prevailing party attorney's fees provision in the contract, the winner will still be out-of-pocket for the attorney's fees, which can be substantial. Sometimes the attorney's fees can even exceed the amount in dispute making it that the person who wins still loses without the prevailing party attorney's fees provision.

Another area you should consider is how success will be measured under an agreement. It is important to define what success means and discuss specific metrics that will be included in the agreement to define success. Instead of leaving it open to interpretation, businesses should make sure there is an objective metric, whether it is "You get a maximum of __ revisions before there are additional charges" or "The website must be able to fulfill a minimum of Y orders per hour." This helps ensure that if a dispute arises later, a third-party can determine whether those objective standards set forth in the contract were met.

For example, a lack of measurable metrics caused problems for a software developer client of ours who had entered into an agreement that required them to "perform to the satisfaction of the customer." Unfortunately, their customer repeatedly changed the scope of the project, which was broadly defined in the initial agreement, and requested numerous change orders. Not only did the scope of changes cost my client over one hundred thousand dollars in lost developer's fees, but also their customer alleged that my client had not performed to their satisfaction. Displeased, the customer requested a full refund from my client.

Useful objective metrics are determined by considering the expectations of all sides before entering into an agreement. In addition to customer agreements between a business and their customers, partner agreements for new businesses can become contentious if the owners do not think through the potential issues in advance. Agreements are an opportunity to put into writing each side's expectations and responsibilities before someone feels unappreciated, under compensated, or ill-used. For example, a partner agreement should define how profits and losses are going to be allocated. If the business is profitable, then the issues usually take care of themselves, but many founders do not consider what happens if things do not go as projected, including how losses will be allocated, whether partners can be required to invest additional capital into the business if needed, and what happens if a partner refuses to invest additional capital to keep the business operational. To resolve this and other potential problems, one approach I recommend to my clients it to create a list of the most likely disputes that they foresee occurring and to consider their ideal solutions before they enter into any kind of agreement. I ask them to do this because risk is far easier to allocate while it is still only hypothetical.

In that regard, you must be cautious about ensuring that everything they think you are agreeing to is included in the written agreement before you sign it. Sometimes, especially when businesses are in their early stages, business owners will say to me, "Well, the person told me that we had the deal, even though it is not in the agreement. They told me that I can trust them, and it is going to be fine." The problem with that kind of thinking is contracts typically include an integration clause that specifically says that the written agreement is the entire agreement and that it supersedes any prior written or oral agreements about that subject matter. Put simply, the integration clause means that regardless of what was discussed in the negotiations leading to the written agreement, if the clause is not in the written agreement, then it is not a part of the agreement. There are certain arguments that can be made to get around a clause like that, but to the extent that you can avoid having to look for the exception to the rule, you are much better off including it in the agreement. Otherwise, if there is an integration clause, and lawyers for both sides are preparing to litigate a dispute, it is an almost certainty that one side will argue that the written agreement is the entire agreement.

As a final note on agreements, and in an attempt to help my insurers sleep easier at night, please note that nothing in this chapter is to be construed as forming representation between you and me or my firm or to be acted on without the advice of a well-experienced lawyer. For legal advice, I recommend that you retain a qualified lawyer, such as myself or someone else, and avoid implementing any of these strategies on your own. Nevertheless, hopefully these tips will help you foresee some potential legal problems before they arise. Good luck!

CHAPTER 14

HOW EVERY BUSINESS OWNER CAN WIN GOOGLE MAPS RANKINGS ETHICALLY & ORGANICALLY

By **QAMAR ZAMAN**

In my years of practicing and honing my skills as a digital growth marketer, first as a practitioner and now as a coach and consultant, I have developed a unique, proven science for digital marketing and discovered specific indicators that either makes a business owner very successful or causes them to fail miserably. When a business owner or entrepreneur applies my predictable growth plan, they will grow exponentially. So, let's not waste any more time!

My strategic framework for digital marketing is broken into five small modules that make up the acronym CAROM:

C - Current situation
A - Aim
R - Ritual
O - Options
M - Method

Let me explain the above with some examples.

C - Current situation

Where are you in terms of your digital marketing plan? If your current situation is that you only get ten website leads per month and you are converting those into sales, you need to write that down as your current reality. Most business owners don't actually have the faintest idea of how their website is performing; if that rings true for you, then you're already at a disadvantage with no way to know the source of your leads.

A - Aim

Where do you want to go? Without knowing where you want to go, you can't map the direction forward. When I consult with clients, I start out by asking them what their aim is for the future. I want to find out precisely what they want in terms of sales per month or sales per year.

Being on the first page of Google for some keywords is hopefully not your aim. It is a means to an aim, but it should not be your overall goal. We will need to build a blueprint for growth to prepare a plan to get you the growth you want. With these details in mind, we can go after a specific result.

R - Ritual

How will you get there? Rituals are the specific, measurable, attainable, realistic, and time-bound (SMART) routines or strategies that build a lead generation machine and will yield predictable results every single day.

O - Options and Methods

These are the golden frameworks and tactical methods that are built and deployed to keep the lead machine running and get results, which creates a profit faucet for every business owner. A golden framework is made of up different options including your website, landing pages, Google search engine optimization, Google paid advertising, Google map, Mobile apps, Youtube, Facebook, LinkedIn, Twitter, and Instagram. Tactical methods are various processes to achieve the desired results, called conversion touchpoints, where money exchanges happen.

Since it is hard to put all the components of a golden framework in one place, I have provided a blueprint that every business owner, whether they operate a brick-and-mortar storefront or a virtual business, can use to monetize their business using Google Maps. In this chapter, I outline step-by-step plans to rank your business on the first page of Google's search results using Google Maps. Since the ranking factors of search engines change constantly, I will keep this resource evergreen.

At the time of writing, I have helped over 1,450 small business owners achieve significant results from my systems. Those who followed my plan completely achieved exponential growth. *Online Resource: Kisspr.com/gmb*

How To Rank and Win Google Maps Ethically and Organically

In the digital era, the market is no longer restricted to conventional mediums like print, radio and Yellow Pages or the local market. To ensure a healthy share in the market, it is mandatory that business owners take all measures to increase brand awareness amongst their target audience, through any and all means possible.

If you want to boost your sales and stay ahead of your competition, the digital sphere is the first place you should focus on establishing a robust presence.

These days, it is all about making use of big data to better understand your customers and market your brand. If you are a local business owner with limited resources or a midsize enterprise looking to expand your customer base, then this chapter has the perfect solution for you.

When it comes to searching for anything online, we are all aware of Google's dominance and ability to continually evolve. To ensure their own success, Google strives to make everyone happy. According to Statista, it is ranked as the most visited multi-platform web property with 246 million users in the United States alone. This statistic demonstrates the popularity of the search engine among Americans.

Google also offers multiple services and tools for helping business owners market goods and services in a more efficient manner. Results are not solely dependent on the size of your budget. I recommend that business owners focus on smarter spending. With Google, less can be more. As a result, Google Maps rankings has become one of the best ways to expand your customer base and make your business successful in the long run.

What Is Google My Business and Why Should You Care?

Google My Business (GMB) is an essentially free website and what I refer to as your "Golden Frame." Acting as an interface and extension of Google, it allows you as a business owner or entrepreneur to take the reins regarding how your business will be displayed on all Google platforms. It also provides visiting users with a brief about your company and offers social proof (i.e., customer reviews) it has received from the customers. Utilizing GMB is a powerful way to improve your business's local visibility.

Today, no matter what industry your business competes in, online visibility is a must to retain a successful business. When you utilize GMB service, it establishes your business online and you get a claim for the GMB page. Once you have claimed or verified the page, you should make the best use of the online presence by optimizing the listing. Eventually, your business will get a higher ranking on Google Maps and search engines.

To help you with the process, I have developed a predictable growth strategy for the maintenance of your GMB page. A well-maintained and diligently optimized GMB page will grow and boost your presence on Google search results, and it will also increase the search engine visibility of your business. So, let's get started with the steps!

Step One: Know Your Audience

You will be unable to make any marketing technique successful unless you treat your customer as the ultimate beneficiary. If your customers are happy, your business will boom. So, the first step to making your brand stick and stand out to your audience means you will need to actually understand your audience. No matter what search engine marketing you decide to employ, each strategy should be designed in a way that allows your business to be found by your audience.

You may ask, "How will I know who is in my audience?" It shouldn't be surprising to find that the answer to this question lies with Google. It has several tools and services that can provide you with adequate insight into the online behavior of your audience. You can access a free tool by Google called Keyword Planner through a Google Ads account. This tool can help you find keywords that users are using to search for particular words or phrases that are relevant to your business.

For instance, if you are a lawyer based in Michigan, you can check multiple keywords like: "Michigan lawyer," "lawyer in Michigan," "legal help, Michigan," "law firm near me in Michigan." Google's Keyword Planner tool will give you insight into how often these words are used in your targeted area. This way, you will know what sort of keywords you can use in your content and on your page to improve its ranking.

Online Resource: Why is this important? To be found on Google for your target audience, you need to add metadata and understand how Google works. More on this topic *(Kisspr.com/gmb)*

Step Two: Build Your GMB Page

Technically, building your GMB page should be the first step in the process. I have listed it as the second step deliberately to emphasize that your first priority must be to understand your audience. Only then will you be able to develop a GMB page that is efficient and relevant.

To get your GMB page, register your business and set up an account. You can claim your current business page. When you pursue a GMB site for claiming your business, it shows you a listing of businesses. You will need to enter the most basic and extremely accurate information about your business. Doing this ensures that your business details do not overlap with any other existing company and that your individuality is maintained. You'll know whether or not your business is in the listing.

You'll be asked to complete the information related to your business and the nature of its service. Make sure your answers are accurate, comprehensive, and free of grammatical errors. When you choose the option of business categories, pick the one that is the most relevant to your service. Remember you can always edit the information, and it's important to regularly monitor and update information as it changes.

I recommend that you select only one relevant category. For example, if you are a personal injury lawyer, select "Personal Injury Attorney." In our online version of this book, we dive into this example in more detail with images and video. *Check it out here: (Kisspr.com/gmb)*

Once you have created your account, the second stage in this process is verifying your GMB listing. This step is imperative for your online visibility. Once you've created the account, Google will mail a postcard directly to the mailing address you provided during your account setup. Receiving this postcard is crucial to verify your business; without it, you can't access your GMB page. Receiving the postcard may take a week's time. Now your business is live!

Step Three: Optimize Your GMB Page

Once your business page is live, the next step is optimizing your GMB page. Optimization plays an instrumental role in boosting online visibility. It helps you attract a significant number of visitors. Efficient optimization brings relevant, quality traffic to your website.

To optimize your website, start by working on analyzing your page's information. Make sure you have accurate details in your profile. You don't want tech users on your website looking for iPhones and macOS when you're actually an apple farmer, do you?

Choose your business category carefully by stating exactly the nature of your business and the market you deal in. You'll only get relevant traffic if you've mentioned the right details.

Your ranking on Google Maps also gets directly influenced by the website URL of your Google business page. Google uses your website to make associations with Google Maps listings. It utilizes elements such as "keyword target" and "business category relevance" to compare with user's queries, and these associations will impact your overall ranking.

This makes it necessary for you to optimize the homepage of your website. Careful keyword selection is the foundation of effective optimization. Choose the keywords that are relevant to your business category and relevant to your audience. Once you have chosen the right keywords, the second most important thing to do is consider where you place them on your homepage.

The best way to see top ranking on Google Maps is by placing the keywords in significant locations. Title tags, description tags, onsite content, and citations are primary locations to consider. If you are a California-based financial planner, for example, Google can give you a higher ranking if your title tag says "Fischer Financial Planning California | Your Wealth Deserves a Plan." This tag immediately shows the basics of your business, and your business name, domain, and area of practice are clearly stated.

Similarly, having the keywords placed in the description and content gives your GMB landing page more relevance. When you place keywords in certain locations, it makes it easier for Google to pull data and give the page a better ranking.

Besides keywords, you should also ensure your website remains updated and offers a productive experience to the user. Keep the basic information, including your business name, address, and contact details, visible to the viewer on every page.

Utilize a content marketing strategy to ensure you are posting fresh content to your website's blog that uses your targeted keywords. Taking the time for this step will have a positive impact on your online visibility. Optimization is all about making your GMB page relevant and user-friendly. Once you are able to keep it efficiently optimized, you'll see a boost in your business's position on Google Maps rankings. *Online Resource: Online Video Resource: Kisspr.com/gmb)*

Step Four: Cater to Diverse Mediums

Optimizing your GMB page for multiple devices can help you receive a higher ranking on Google Maps. According to CIO Dive, up to 70% of web traffic happens on mobile devices, which makes it a necessity for your website to have a competent and responsive design for mobile users.

Implementing a mobile-friendly design, often referred to as responsive web design, allows an easier browsing experience and will automatically adjust to any device it is accessed through by the user.

Accelerated Mobile Pages (AMPs) is an initiative developed by Google to help you create more mobile-friendly web content and improve your search engine ranking. Once you've implemented the AMP markup, your business will be included in Google's search engine results pages (SERPs) and your listing will sometimes appear even higher than the paid advertising results.

Be sure to remove unnecessary content from the page to improve the mobile user's experience. This includes eliminating blank spaces, along with irrelevant content and media. Pages with heavy content take more time to load, negatively affecting the user experience. To decrease website load time, keep a simple design and include only highly relevant content to your business. If you are developing or updating your web design, make sure to add only high-quality images because in today's world they are mandatory for user engagement. Compressed images take up less space and make it a win-win situation for both you and the user.

When working on a mobile-friendly design for your GMB page, incorporating data in a structured manner can give you surprising results. There are plug-ins that allow you to structure your data in a manner that whenever a query is searched by the user, your website can emerge among the top results and outrank other websites. *Online Video Resource: (Kisspr.com/gmb)*

Step Five: Cultivate Niche Business Citations

A citation is any mention of your business name, address, or phone number on any other website. It can be listed on any online source that has a high Local SEO Authority level. Regarding local domination, citations play a huge role in improving your position. The local SEO citations boost your website's authority and, as a result, your SERP rankings increase within the targeted location.

Citations validate your business and increase your credibility for local searches. The format in which you offer your business information contributes to the reliability factor for the search engines as they filter through the internet. When you offer complete data about your business, it assures search engines that you are a legitimate business. Hence, your listing is rewarded above other search results.

Business citations have a greater impact when it comes to the factors influencing the local ranking. However, there are certain aspects that play an important role in determining a positive contribution of a business citation in SEO efforts. First, you are likely to have a higher rank than your competitors if you have more citations than they do. Second, Google has more confidence in the citations from trustworthy and well-indexed sites. So, ensure that you choose the sites carefully for citations. Third, it is important to have citations with the local authority of the location where you're targeting. For instance, having your citation mentioned on Yelp can help boost your local visibility.

To improve your ranking on Google Maps through citations, ensure that all your citations are consistent. They must be in the same sequence with the same address and phone number used to register and verify your GMB page.

When you have your citations on a variety of trusted sites, it shows that you are part of a community, which is something Google appreciates and rewards by improving your ranking in the search results. *Online Video Resource: (Kisspr.com/gmb)*

Step Six: Social Proof (Reviews)

Happy customers are key to a successful business, and you'll only be able to retain happy customers if you make them feel valued. The easiest way to do this is by encouraging them to offer feedback and considering what they say.

When it comes to Google Maps rankings, feedback and reviews are of tremendous value. While there are a lot of other factors involved in search rankings, customer reviews can help your business appear trustworthy to customers. They can give you a significant competitive edge and raise your visibility in the search results. According to Robert B. Cialdini in his 1984 book *Influence: How and Why People Agree To Things*, "social proof," otherwise known as informational social influence, describes a psychological and social phenomenon wherein people copy the actions of others in an attempt to conform.

Google looks for certain signals to help the search engine decide whether or not your site is worth a rise in ranking. Reviews are an endorsement from customers that assures the search engines about your website. They confirm that not only is your business legitimate, but it is approved by the customers too. As a reward for your legitimacy, you are given better visibility.

Now what matters is how you manage these reviews. It is important that you know when and where they appear. There are several review sites like Yelp and TripAdvisor that sends you a notification whenever a user reviews your page. You can also have a paid service for online reputation monitoring. Your GMB page is another place customers can offer a review. To maintain your credibility, you must monitor all reviews and give quality responses.

When replying to reviews, it is important to have a strong customer service attitude, which demonstrates your professionalism. The writing style needs to be friendly. Writing stoically can offend customers. You have to make the customer feel valued for taking time out of their day to offer you their feedback.

Reviews can be positive or negative, and you have to deal with both of them carefully. The staff member responding to the reviews must have the authority to resolve the complaints. This will give problem-resolving quality to your service, making a positive contribution to your online reputation.

Negative reviews can be fearsome. They can affect your Google Maps ranking substantially and create a negative image of your business to potential customers. But if you know how to manage negative reviews, you will be able to avoid the associated pitfalls.

It is a known fact that a healthy amount of reviews are unauthentic. Agencies are paid to write good or bad reviews for companies all the time. If you receive a bad review, it could be that your competitor is carrying out a campaign to tarnish your online image. Therefore, you have to take measures that can filter out fake reviews.

You can do this by encouraging the reviewers to post using their real names when giving reviews. You can also evaluate the language and tone used in the reviews to determine whether or not they are authentic.

For instance, a review that contains overly-negative words and bashing is likely fake. If a large number of negative reviews are posted within a short period of time, it indicates a deliberate attempt to sabotage your company's reputation and lower your online ranking.

For legitimate negative reviews, shape a careful response that acknowledges their feedback and demonstrates that you care about their experience. Managing reviews of your company is a skill. If you know how to handle them correctly, they can play a significant role in bringing your business to the top of Google Maps rankings. *Online Video Resource: Kisspr.com/gmb*

Step Seven: Remain Active for Predictable Growth

The final step toward making your business lead in the Google Maps rankings is to retain a robust online presence. Keeping your website updated with fresh content and optimally-positioned key-words can help you improve your ranking on Google Maps and stay there.

Content comes in multiple forms. You can set up a blog and post relevant articles regularly with the right keywords to signal to Google that your website is updated frequently. You can also share the experience of your customers to boost user engagement on your page and offer insight into the goods or services you offer.

Remain consistent in your posting. Having an active blog is the easiest way to keep your website current and relevant. You can draft a schedule for posting updates or blogs, and then stick to it. Google appreciates consistency and creativity. It will ultimately improve your ranking on all of its platforms if you are successful in assuring the search engines that your content is relevant to the readers.

Getting a high ranking on Google Maps is achieved through strategically planned content and a regularly maintained website. If you are able to optimize your site in a manner favored by Google that is also easy for users to browse, then retaining a higher ranking will not be a challenge for you.

The only requirement to fulfill this strategy is remaining consistent in your efforts to improve your ranking. Tracking and maintaining your business listings on the GMB page can guarantee you a higher online position.

The content you post on your website should relate to your target audience. It should provide users with the right answers. If you are able to accomplish this, you'd be ultimately able to dominate the Google Maps ranking easily.

With this free tool from Google, anyone can follow this plan and achieve organic dominance for any kind of business within Google's terms of service. In my career with digital growth strategies and developing my own press release distribution service, I have helped over 28,000 business owners by using these growth hacks. If you are a visual learner or need step-by-step tactical steps, follow this online resource which will be kept evergreen for readers of this book. I offer my heart's deepest appreciation and gratitude for taking time out of your busy day to read this chapter, and I promise you that if you follow this program on your own or with my help, you will grow your business.

Qamar Zaman
Your Digital Growth Guide | Forbes Member |
www.KissPr.com
https://en.wikipedia.org/wiki/SMART_criteria

CHAPTER 15

HOW TO LEVEL UP YOUR LEADERSHIP

By **REGINA NEWBERRY**

"Identify your problems but give your power and energy to solutions."
– Anonymous

Imagine a budding young woman who recently graduated from a prestigious university. She's eager, fresh, and excited, yet green in her profession. Even so, she lands her first job right out of college. Let's say her name is Beth.

Beth jumps right into her profession and gleans all that she can, like a sponge.

However, there's a huge issue lurking about her career. Any time she attempts to share creative ideas, she's ignored, looked over, or someone steals them without giving credit to her. Beth ignores it for years and wonders why her bosses do not take her seriously. Initially, to combat the feeling of being devalued and unappreciated, she achieves a higher degree and works longer hours but she was still treated the same. Eventually, she becomes numb and silent. She refrains from sharing ideas, ones that could have possibly saved the company lots of money. She was a top performer but not acknowledged as one. Finally, she doesn't care anymore and resigns.

A Call to Action

Why doesn't her management respect, appreciate, or allow her to share valuable input? Can you calculate the cost of her not being engaged or the cost to the company when she resigned?

Don't allow the next Oprah Winfrey or tech giant to walk away from your company because it lacked the ability to tap into the skills and talents of the entire workforce. Instead, this is the time and the era to Level Up. I'm referring to Leveled Up Leadership. This is defined as leaders who realize they must grow, expand by relinquishing traditional mindsets , and become great in order to advance their teams in business.

Before we go a step further, let's expose the top seven issues that cause many organizations to lose unnecessary profits. I'm convinced that many companies really do not understand the full impact of loss profits of this manner. Every issue is tied to management.

The issues are:

1. **Underutilized employee skills** (talents left untouched). When associates aren't challenged, their skills collect dust or become dormant.
2. **Lack of employee engagement and motivation.** This occurs when employees have no passion or energy to go beyond what is being directly asked of them.
3. **Team complacency.** This occurs when associates feel as though their only purpose at work is to collect paychecks. A successful team should be one in which each employee

shares ideas and capitalizes on each other's ideas. In teams like this, innovative brilliance happens.

4. **Antiquated processes and systems.** Many organizations are still using old systems and manual processes in a digital world. This is not efficient or effective for employees.
5. **Lack of management training.** Many leaders are promoted on the basis of how well they do their job, but they are not properly trained on how to lead people. A recent study by CareerBuilder.com shows that a whopping 58% of managers said they didn't receive any management training.
6. **Generation gaps.** There is a generation gap that causes a lack of harmony between Baby Boomers, Gen Xers, and Millennials. They all engage differently, yet they need each other. There is little focus or attention given to this. It takes a leader to bring everyone into alignment.
7. **Lack of employee appreciation.** Global studies reveal that 79% of people who quit their jobs cite 'lack of appreciation' as their reason for leaving. Management must show appreciation to their staff or they will quit.

Let's discuss why it's difficult to resolve these issues.

Honestly, these issues are multi-layered challenges without any emphasis on the dollar figure of profits loss related to employee turnover or potential profit increase that is available but not discovered. I'm referencing monies left on the table. Who can afford the waste? Not to mention the time, efforts in training, and relationships that must be reestablished with clients when someone resigns or is disengaged. This cost is enormous. It's very disruptive to the flow of business and it's a vicious cycle that must be broken.

The above issues have a negative effect. Profit loss is often the result of high turnover rates and/or low or absent employee engagement. According to the Bureau of Labor Statistics, the employee turnover rate was 43%. The Bureau also stated that from 2015 to 2018 there was 5.6 million hires but 5.4 million separations.

According to a 2018 Gallup poll, 85% of people are not happy with their jobs. Every couple of years, Gallup releases polls that show that nearly 70% of employees are actively disengaged. There is a huge cost associated with disengaged workers.

According to a May 2019 article in the Washington Post, 71% of U.S. workers are looking for a new job. Why are most U.S. workers seeking new employment? Most people quit their bosses and not the company.

According to an article on the LinkedIn blog, the top reason people resign is a lack of opportunities to advance (45%). The other biggest reasons people resign included unhappiness with leadership (41%), unhappiness with the work environment (36%), and a desire for more challenging work (36%).

A report issued by the Work Institute states that the successful economy and growing job marketplace allow a large percentage of employees to make career moves when their current employers are not meeting their expectations or needs. The Work Institute also estimated that 42 million (or one in four) employees left their jobs in 2018 and that nearly 77% of that turnover could be prevented by employers.

The Work Institute reveals the most important reasons employees decided to leave their jobs. They grouped the reasons into ten categories, seven of which are considered preventable by employers. Is this due to employers not having the ability to identify the root causes? Why do employers give so little attention to such useful statistical data?

Employee turnover costs employers money. According to the Work Institute report, employers spent at least $600 billion in turnover costs in 2018 and can expect that number to increase to $680 billion by the year 2020. Let's face it: employees have options, and multiple studies show that they are not hesitant to leave their current positions for jobs that are better fits.

Employee turnover is so expensive because organizations pay direct exit costs when an employee leaves and incur additional costs to recruit and train new hires. Direct exit costs can include payouts for accrued vacation time and unused sick time, contributions to healthcare coverage, higher unemployment taxes, and severance pay. Side effects of turnover, such as decreased productivity, knowledge loss, and lowered morale, can incur incidental costs, as well.

And I know what you're thinking, I don't have a high turnover rate. My questions then would simply be: are your employees fully engaged and working with a purpose beyond just performing daily tasks? Are you truly aware of your team's condition?

According to an article published in Forbes, recognition is the number one thing employees say that their manager could give them to inspire them to produce great work. Studies have proven that when it comes to inspiring people to be their best at work, nothing else comes close--not even higher pay, promotion, increased autonomy, or additional training. (Do me a favor and don't ask a sales team about higher pay not being their first priority!)

Solutions

Many sweeping trends will inform your approach to reducing turnover and improving employee engagement; every company is different. All companies, however, should hire someone without bias to look at your data, whether that's turnover metrics or employee surveys. They will help you understand and address the causes of turnover and lack of motivation.

Partner with a management consulting team to improve performance and productivity. They are available to assist in the execution process. Be determined to transform challenges into opportunities. Profits are at stake!

Focus on continuous improvement to attack one issue after the next to stay ahead of the curve. There is a curve and it must be acknowledged. The curve is like a tsunami that has suddenly overtaken businesses and the sad part is no one ever saw it coming. It's here, so prepare as a leader would.

Become a disruptor by challenging the traditional leadership methods that do not work in this day and age.

Learn leadership tactics that are nontraditional. Servant Leadership is an example that calls for focused attention on employees by making sure they have the updated tools required to do their job with excellence.

Create a movement in the workforce culture. Work culture should be strategically planned and executed. Employees wish to belong to something with purpose and fulfillment.

Look at emotional intelligence skills to add to your leadership toolkit. Here are five skills:

1. **Self-awareness**
2. **Self-management**
3. **Empathy or the ability to see things from employees' perspectives**
4. **Skillful navigation of work relationships.**
5. **The ability to motivate others**

A great leader zones in with the team with an emphasis on exceptional customer service-internal and external. This works for all industries. It all ties to organizational development starting with leaders.

Hence, if your organization has a desire for your supervisors to Level Up, the opportunity is available. It's possible to become great and grow your business by retaining your best asset – THE PEOPLE. Get a higher return on investment (ROI) by developing as a leader, which will thereby enhance the team. As a leader you must learn the type of transferable skills, such as a servant, leader, and coach.

In my book *Recognizing a Cash Cow: Honing In on Your Company's Best Asset – THE PEOPLE*, I advise leaders to use the skills similar to a coach of a sports team. In order to make the team great or develop dream teams, the leader or coach must know the strengths and weaknesses of every player. It's called building relationships and managing skills and talents.

The Leveled Up Leader must have an eye to develop their teams which is in alignment with the yearly targets. Leaders should create work in order to blossom their teams which requires ambitions greater than the job itself. Why? Employees wish to belong to something bigger than their daily tasks. I'm alluding to creating a winning culture.

Finally, I'd like to leave you with this story, also mentioned in my book. Steve Jobs, the visionary who led Apple, did not invent the iPhone. But he challenged his design team and they delivered big. How many people do you know with iPhones?

I'm convinced that with the right leadership training, leaders will have the capability to unearth the talents and gifts that are planted in every employee. I'm certain there are cash cows or overachievers waiting and wanting to be challenged. There are opportunities and innovations planted in every associate that are eagerly awaiting to be unleashed by you, the leader!

Therefore, set yourself apart and become a distinguished, effective leader. It's possible to create dream teams in corporate America as in the sports industry. As leaders, it's your responsibility to take action and look for ways to promote positive change.

This is a Leveled Up Leader! Leaders are responsible for inspiring the best in people; it starts with changing the way bosses manage today. Be one of the first to save billions of profits from the unnecessary hindrances of high employee turnover and disengaged employees.

With updated and improved training for bosses to become transformed into effective leaders, a top performer like Beth would not only be retained; but flourishing. The gold or talent is in the employee. Therefore, when leaders properly engage their associates, many organizations will decrease high turnover rates and undesired high profit losses. Also, they will have the tools to discover potential profit increases by way of their dream teams. Who's ready to keep avoidable loss profits? Then get the resources required to become a Leveled Up Leader.

CHAPTER 16

TECHNOLOGY PRIVATE EQUITY DONE RIGHT

By **DR. RIADH FAKHOURY**

At some point everyone has had the experience of losing money while making investments. Perhaps the loss was emotionally upsetting, or maybe you lost money in a deal with a family member or trusted friend. Usually, such a loss causes a high level of fear about investing again. Fear, along with uncertainty, can paralyze you and prevent you from investing again, resulting in lost financial growth.

Listen, it is okay to have lost. No matter how hurtful, emotionally scarring or great the amount of the loss; no matter if you have lost money once, twice or even several times - it is actually a positive thing.

Remember when you learned how to ride a bike? What if you stopped trying after the first or second fall? You would have never learned the art, skill and joy of bicycle riding. You would have lost out on that special experience. Imagine how life would have been if your own fear had caused you to lose that opportunity for freedom, and the ability to go when and where you wanted to.

Similar to falling down when learning to ride a bicycle, it is okay to invest and lose money – even a lot of it! Do not give up on investing. Learn from your mistakes and move ahead to become a better investor. The key to learning is watching and mimicking those who are successful and repeating the process until you get it right.

Alternatively, if you choose not to invest, you will miss out on the bounties altogether as well as wonderful and life-changing opportunities that come with that success. Don't miss out.

Here's another point to think about: once proficient in riding a bike, did you ever have another fall? You most likely you did. However, subsequent falls have a tendency to be less dramatic and less hurtful than the first falls. Therefore, the art and skill of private equity investing is like riding a bike.

If you pay attention and follow consistent procedures and steps, you will have more success than failure. Remember that positive outcomes and success is simply having more of the good than the not-so-good.

Let go of the emotional hurt or fear and learn that investing is an active game with rules and steps to follow. The closer you stay on the right path, the more success you will gain.

What Is Private Equity Investment and Why Should You Consider It?

Private equity represents a sector of investment where capital funds are placed into privately held companies and investors have direct ownership in the company. Participation can include many areas such as real estate, manufacturing, retail and technology. My personal focus and passion in private investing is the technology sector.

Imagine ownership in a space where the innovations of a company can literally change an entire industry! Risks are high in private equity investment, but the probability of loss can be reduced significantly by following simple and clear rules of business. We will discuss several of these rules that will help to mitigate the risk of loss, allowing investors to make wise decisions as to how and when to participate in private equity.

Done correctly, an entrepreneurial investor can participate successfully in the private equity space, owning a piece of the company and taking advantage of potential high returns.

Mechanism and Life of a Start-Up

A start-up is just that – an idea and excitement that is born. Founders then surround themselves with angel investors who participate in early stage rounds of investment, called "seed" rounds, to incubate the company. The company should then grow through stages in technology and staff. Like anything, start-ups need support in the form of cash to continue to grow. If successful, its life cycle can be as short as two years or as long as 10 years.

This is where the important part comes in. The secret to a successful start-up is actually not determined by the product or service itself – there are so many great ideas out there that never make it. What determines a start-up's loss or gain is the company's management team on the inside, and the board of directors on the outside who direct the company's management team.

If there is a strong internal team (that may include a CEO and founders), a highly experienced and resourceful board of directors, coupled with an excellent, disruptive product in a specific niche and in a space that has strong market relevance, then you have the ingredients for great success.

We have touched on some important criteria that need to be in place to reduce the chances of "falling off your bike" again. Notice that the above recipe is not an investment commercial on TV, or a friend telling you about their last big win and coaxing you to do the same. Done correctly, you can become your own successful financial planner.

Remember, there are three big requirements to follow for success:

1. Make sure you are aligned with the best in the industry. In this case, align yourself with the experts of private equity investments in technology start-ups.
2. Make sure that these experts have skin in the game. Will the board, founders and CEO lose money or their reputation if there is a failure?
3. These experts must also have a reverse relationship of risk to reward on investment outcomes. The track record of success and wins must be much, much greater than the losses.

This is the recipe for success, but how often will you have the components of your investment opportunities line up like this? Not very often.

This is where the secret of a successful private equity company, such as Vestech Partners, that follows these important requirements and principles, becomes so significant. Vestech Partners is our personal, family-owned investment company that presents investors with a vehicle to participate in exclusive and restricted technology investment opportunities.

Let's continue on.

Optimum Valuation for Optimum Outcomes, Reducing Risk and Producing Maximum Returns

The beginning of a start-up's life is important. Many start-ups become overvalued from the very beginning. They take on too much money. Their eyes are bigger than their stomachs. This results in a poor start, and it can result in a negative outcome for your investment.

To get the money it needs, a young start-up company, with a great idea or product, may go to an institutional or venture capitalist investor. These investors often finance large sums of money into the company. Understanding the risk of investment at this stage in the game is high, these institutional investors usually demand a large chunk of ownership in the start-up and request a seat on the board to maintain control. Now you have a start-up company glutted with money, overvalued and run like a government. This is a recipe for a big fall off the bicycle.

Let's then imagine that this early start-up begins to move ahead and thus needs additional capital investment. Where will this money come from? Usually not the institutional investors. Those investors already own a large portion of the company and investing more would gain them management control of the company. So, the inside management team - which may include the founders and CEO - turn to private equity investors.

Unfortunately for them, the company is already overvalued. Who in their right mind would want to put their hard-earned money into a company that is over-priced, and will have a reduced outcome when sold? When a start-up tries to attract private equity, for its own survival, it might do a down round or undervalue the company.

This essentially means the valuation of the company, or the expectation of everyone working hard within the company, is reduced below its original amount. Psychologically, this causes the troops within the company to become very unhappy and can lead to the beginning of the end.

Therefore, it is imperative to have the right leadership controlling the initial valuation of the company. This leadership will keep valuation reasonable, and will add incremental and controlled increases to that valuation as additional private equity funds come in.

This control of valuations allows investors to have a much better outcome upon the sale or initial public offering (IPO) of the company. Remember, a lower valuation of the company reflects as a greater return on investment (ROI) when the company is sold.

For example: if a home sells for $200,000 USD, the investor's return is greater if their original investment was made at a valuation of $100,000 compared to $150,000.

If a company is glutted with funds and has a high valuation, walk away. Initial controlled valuation, along with incremental and controlled funding commensurate with the company's growth, will result in a much better outcome.

Special Purpose Vehicles and How They Work

A special purpose vehicle (SPV) is a limited liability corporation (LLC) that has a specific purpose wherein a group of investors come together to invest their money in some entity, such as a start-up company or a real estate project.

The SPV should have an operating and stock equity agreement. These documents will clearly delineate how the entity functions, including: 1) who is in charge; 2) where the investment monies will be placed; 3) how the funds are to be distributed; 4) how shares are sold in different situations; 5) what the price-per-share is; 6) who the owners of the company are; 7) and many more details on issues that may arise.

For example, Vestech Partners is the manager for multiple special purpose vehicles. Vestech Partners brings deals to the investors, hires experienced United States Security and Exchange Commission attorneys, has an accounting staff, negotiates the best deals for the investors and vets deals to ensure the best outcomes for the least amount of risk.

For these services, Vestech Partners collects an annual management fee of two percent, and collects 20 percent of profit upon sale or exit of the company. Vestech Partners protects its investors and represents its commitment to success by placing a written protection to investors, whereby Vestech Partners will waive its 20 percent back-end fee if a certain threshold of profit - usually 100 percent - is not realized by the investors.

Not All Private Equity Deals Are Equal

There is a reason why private equity investments in the technology world fail so often. Many intricacies need to fall accurately into place for a company to become successful. The opportunity must be properly vetted from multiple analytic angles.

The following questions are necessary to consider before investing:

1. What will be the source of funding?
2. How much money will the company take in?
3. Does the founder or CEO have the leadership skills and qualities to take the company through the many stages and challenges ahead?

These, and many other questions, must be addressed and handled to reduce the risk of failure.

It has become clear to me that there is a plethora of fantastic ideas and innovations. Again, the success of a company is not based on such ideas and innovations, but rather on its management team and board who should be seasoned and experienced to properly guide the company through the challenges that it will face.

Proper leadership is of the utmost importance. These leaders will be able to bring solutions, resources and experience to the table when the company has a major internal or external obstacle to deal with. These obstacles can include competition, lack of funding, deal flow, product development or even loss of a key internal member.

A strong management and leadership team will allow for a clear and uninterrupted execution of the product, development, uniqueness, innovation, marketing, building of a customer base and generation of income while maintaining a reasonable valuation and needed funding. Any disruption of this balance will increase the opportunity for the company to spiral downward.

Having excellent, experienced and resourceful leadership is a major key to success. Great ideas are all around; seeing them to fruition requires the right team. Vestech Partners associates itself with only the best, most experienced and most resourceful teams.

Not All Private Equity Managers Are Created Equally

Private equity managers bring opportunities for your review. The key to finding the right manager is to understand from whom and where they get their deal flow, or pipeline of investment opportunities.

Are they doing their own homework, or do they have a credible inside source guiding and advising them? If they have a source, is he or she well-connected and experienced in the space of the start-up technology world? Are these sources that recommend the opportunities personally involved in the investments monetarily and carrying a leadership role? Do these advisors have a proven and outstanding track record of success while maintaining minimal losses?

The private equity manager must have a robust pipeline of the highest-quality deal flow, otherwise it's just a guessing game and a wish for success. It is also important to consider the terms of investment that are being presented by the private equity manager.

Has the private equity manager been able to negotiate excellent terms to secure the investors? Is there a floor, or downside mechanism, to protect the investors in the case of an emergency liquidation of the company? What rights does the investor group have? What are the terms of the note, or the financial agreement containing the investment details, between the company and the investors? How well can the private equity manager protect its investor group?

Be sure to check into the following regarding your private equity manger and the deals being presented to you:

1. The private equity manager should have the resources and ability to find exclusive opportunities for investors.
2. He or she should have a track record of being affiliated and working with the most experienced, successful and resourceful advisors.
3. The private equity firm should have strong relationships with the board and CEO where they are awarded to lead the round. Leading a round puts the private equity company in charge of collecting funds, and the autonomy on deciding which investor can participate in the opportunity.
4. Finally, the manager should also have enough influence and experience to set terms that are beneficial to the investors, have an impressive track record and be capable of clearly determining which deals he or she believes are winners.

Getting Started

One of the most challenging components of investing is pulling the trigger - committing yourself to move money from a personal account into an investment.

Many people will do all of the homework, study the risk and be ready to move ahead, only to get stuck and avoid moving forward with the final stage. Quite often, the investor will not move ahead because they are afraid due to past experiences of losses and failures.

It is important to note that failure is just as important, if not more so, than success. It is the failure that teaches you what not to do, and how to invest more effectively the next time around.

If the pieces of the investment puzzle fit and make sense, as discussed in this chapter, and the investor is keen on participating, then it is imperative that he or she put aside their fears and move forward. If not, the opportunity and excitement of being part of a revolutionary technology will be lost and go to someone else.

All investments have rules that are similar and consistent. Whether it be private equity investing in technology or investments into real estate. Following these rules, as I described above, dramatically reduces the risk of loss. Although you can never eliminate risk completely, following the rules and guidelines will limit your exposure to risk and help you, the investor, move forward and not be left behind.

CHAPTER 17

CELEBRATE THE ORDINARY

By **SCOTT VON DEYLON**

It was a Monday morning in June. The year was 1993. I was ten. I remember it so vividly. All my friends were off having a blast at camp while I was stuck at home in rural Cincinnati, lamenting my summer vacation. I was bored out of my mind. Every. Single. Day. Unless of course, that day happened to be a Monday, because Monday was "caddy day" at Hyde Park Country Club.

Caddies were allowed to play one free, glorious round and I was lucky because my grandfather was a member. Since I secretly dreamed of joining the PGA tour and because I was what one might describe as "lower middle class" or, in less politically correct terms, poor, I would do anything to caddy for my grandfather. He knew it, too, which meant regularly hand-washing his silver Nissan 350Z and cutting grass with a push mower at his house and local church. It was a small price to pay, and I was happy to pay it every damn summer from 1992 through 1999.

But one Monday in June 1993 was different. When my grandfather rolled up to the curb an hour early to pick me up, I had no idea that this day would play a major role in shaping the rest of my life. And the funny thing is, it had absolutely nothing to do with golf.

My First Day in Sales

Before I continue, I should also disclose that I absolutely adored and looked up to my grandfather from the day he entered my life until the day he left it, at least in the physical form. He was my hero.

Back to that morning. After hopping in shotgun, my grandfather casually informed me that I would first be accompanying him to a quick business meeting downtown. I was happy to go. To be honest, I was just thrilled to be out of the house and, besides, it didn't sound like there would be any grass to cut at this business meeting. We drove downtown, parked at a meter, and walked into one of the most majestic buildings on 4th Street, which was once home to the Cincinnati Stock Exchange. I had never been in any building downtown let alone the building downtown. In fact, the only time I had ever even been downtown was when my mom begged my dad to take me to a Reds game. They lost and he complained about the cost of the tickets the whole way home. Suffice it to say, there wasn't a whole lot of father-son bonding that took place that day.

Anyway, my grandfather and I walked through the grandiose archway that opened to reveal large, gold-plated doors and I was immediately captivated. The building had a musky scent of old leather and oak that was oddly intoxicating. I remember the distinct sound of high heels clicking across the white marble floor. Then I looked up and saw the vaulted forty-foot high celling boasting a complex pattern of blue and gold medallions and an impressive collection of archways. Ding! The gold elevator doors opened, and we got in along with a bunch of men in three-piece suits who all looked like very important people doing very important things.

My grandfather pushed the button for the top floor, and we were on our way. After exiting the elevator, we entered an office and he was greeted with a warm smile by the secretary. My grandfather turned to me, pointed to the lobby and told me to wait while he was whisked away into the boardroom. After spending the better part of two hours sitting on an old wooden bench watching the secretary type away at her desk without any TV, tablet, or smart phone to entertain me, I had a revelation that I was fortunate to keep inside the walls of my brain: I could never work here, I could never be a suit. I thought I was bored at home, but this was truly the epitome of boring.

The boardroom doors opened, and another impressive looking man in an even more impressive suit looked right at me and said, "Mr. Von Deylen?" I nodded. Sensing that I may have been a bit overwhelmed--duh--he flashed a toothy smile and said, "Get on in here." I did as I was told. I got up and walked straight into the boardroom where twelve other men, all of whom looked just like him, sat around a large mahogany conference table. My eyes immediately landed on my grandfather who sat on the middle left side, cool as a cucumber. We locked eyes and he gave me a subtle nod and a wink, the subtext of which was, "You're okay, kiddo."

The boss sat me down at the head of the table, put his arm on the back of my chair, and said, "Scott, are you going to take over the business for your grandfather one day?" I froze. My mouth opened, but nothing came out. It was a simple question, and yet I had no response. When it was clear that this question would go unanswered, the boss chided me, "What's wrong, son? Cat got your tongue?" The room erupted in obsequious laughter. I watched as the expression on my grandfather's face quickly turned from pride to disappointment. My stomach dropped.

When the chuckles died down, I managed to work up the courage to proffer an answer, albeit it was in a timid voice that I did not even recognize, "Maybe one day." Satisfied that I was at least capable of speaking English, the boss gave me a parting piece of advice, "Listen to your grandfather, he's a damn good salesman!" Before I could respond, my grandfather, who never let anyone get one over on him, chirped back, "What are you talking about?! You guys are making all the money in this deal!" The room erupted in laughter, this time genuine. He had the suits who had just a moment ago seemed larger than life eating out of the palm of his hand. It was incredible to behold and awe-inspiring. My grandfather wasn't just my hero, he was their hero, too. As I was led around the table to shake hands with all the associates, my grandfather snuck up behind me, gave me a pat on the back, and whispered in my ear, "Let's get the hell outta here and play some golf, eh?" I smiled and nodded.

As my grandfather and I walked back to the elevator, my world went into slow motion. The sounds around me faded to a muted hush. I could feel every beat of my heart. I had been sucked into a world that just a few hours ago I had no idea existed. We exited the elevator and walked across the lobby. My twelve-dollar pair of white grassed-stained sneakers squeaked on the shiny marble floor. I took one more look up at that marvelous ceiling and, in that moment, I made a life-changing decision. Despite having been more nervous and scared than at any other point in my relatively short ten-year existence, I knew that I wanted more. No, I needed more. And from that point on, I was determined to do everything in my power to get more.

The Long and Winding Road

In 2013, I started with PrescribeWellness, a software as a service (SaaS) company. We were very much a startup. With less than thirty clients, the business was in the red, surviving on seed money from the original investors. At the time of my hire as employee number three, I had already worked more than my fair share of odds and ends sales jobs. I sold Volkswagen cars, male enhancement supplements over the phone, Cutco knives, and, my personal favorite, DVDs full of trivia content to activity directors of the nation's more than twenty thousand nursing homes. Over the course of more than ten years in sales, I learned a lot about what worked. But more importantly, I learned everything about what didn't work. Speaking of not working, it was during that period I dabbled in college where I learned that college was a waste of money--at least for me. I also spent twelve weeks in the Marine Corps before being discharged with an irregular heartbeat. Who knew? The Marines sure did. Anyway, this is just a roundabout way of saying that my real sales education took place through a long series of trial and error. I got my ass kicked--on sales calls, in the classroom, on the imaginary battlefield. It was learning how to get back up after defeat that was invaluable.

By the tender age of twenty-eight, I was making solid money as a salesman and I knew that selling, whatever it might be, was what I was put on this earth to do. However, I knew that if I was going to continue along this career path, I needed to find an opportunity in a growing industry that would expose me to a lager network than, say, selling knives, cars, or DVDs to nursing home activity directors would. Plus, I was hungry, over-confident, and ready to make a big change. PrescribeWellness checked all those boxes.

Easy, right? Not exactly. The learning curve was steep, especially considering that I had no healthcare background. But I did have a lot of experience selling and, if I can toot my horn for a second, I was a natural on the phone. And here is something I have since learned:

experience and ability can never be overrated. I'll never forget the day I got the call from our CEO, Al Babbington. I was leaving work in downtown Cincinnati. He asked if I would move to California to lead PrescribeWellness's sales department. To a small town, blue-collar Ohio kid, California was mythical, a state I had only seen in movies and TV shows. As I continued to walk the Cincy streets, Al laid out his vision for me at the company. I thanked him and told him I would think about it and get back to him in a few days.

After we hung up, I knew I had a big decision to make, especially with two young kids and another on the way. As I walked, the gravity of the proposal began to sink in. My mind started to race. Then I suddenly stopped, realizing that I was on 4th Street. I looked up and found myself staring at the two large gold doors belonging to the old Stock Exchange Building that I visited with my grandfather some twenty years earlier. I had not returned to the site since that magical day. In this moment, I knew what I had to do. I walked in. My eyes looked down at that glossy marble floor. I took a deep breath and then looked up at that beautiful celling. I looked out the window and gazed at downtown Cincinnati. Then I sat down on an old wooden bench just like the one I sat on years before. I thought about my life. I thought about my grandfather, who had passed four years earlier. I wiped the tears from eyes, stood up, and headed back out through those gold doors. I took out my phone, called my CEO, and accepted his offer.

The following six years, from 2013 to 2019, would prove to be a wild ride filled with countless accomplishments and many failures. It's the nature of the beast. I went from leading a small sales team in Cincinnati to running an organization's entire sales force, growing the company not only to profitability but to $32 million in annual recurring revenue with current growth at more than $10 million year-over-year. And still growing.

Now, with seventeen years of selling behind me, I have learned certain truths. One is that there is no magic bullet. Selling takes years of hard work and experience--that is what gets results. What worked yesterday may not work today. Never get too low with the lows or too high with the highs. I share my personal story only to prove the greatest sales lesson I have ever learned: everyone has a story to tell and everyone wants to tell their story. The question is, will you listen? If you can get a client or prospect to share their story with you and you are able to understand where they have been and where they are trying to go, you will always have an opportunity to earn their business. Selling is an art, not a science. Having data to show us where the best prospects may reside and deciding the best sales strategy, price point, and content of a presentation are all well and good, but, in the end, it's not what we say, it's how we say it. Having the ability to instantaneously make the appropriate adjustment in any conversation or sales presentation to optimize your chances of closing based on the individual or group you are speaking to is invaluable. Having leadership in place that knows how to coach and implement these techniques while creating a culture that buys in is a recipe for success. That is the true difference between winning and losing sales teams.

The Secret to My Success

Now, what I just laid out above is stuff that any competent salesperson worth their salt should know. Yeah, it's a message I deliver to my teams, but it isn't the message. Remember my grandfather? When I said he shaped my life, I did not mean because he gave me the idea to work in sales. No, he taught me how to successfully work in sales. You see, my grandfather always loved to dole out life advice to anyone who would listen. I didn't realize it then, but they were little magical pearls of wisdom, and they always came when I least expected it. We could be in the middle of debating the best pitchers to ever lace up for our hometown Reds, and he would suddenly stop, look me dead in the eyes, and drop some serious knowledge on me. These nuggets were always followed by the same question, "You understand what I'm trying to say?" I didn't, but I knew enough to know the right answer was, "Yes, Grandpa." Truth is, I wouldn't truly understand until years later, but, as they say, it doesn't matter how you get to the dance just that you get there. And I got there.

Now for the best piece of advice he ever gave me: Always take time to appreciate anything you accomplish no matter how small it might be. In other words, not only is it okay to stop and smell the roses, it's necessary. Over the years, this philosophy has morphed into something of my life's defining motto, both personally and professionally. I call it 'Celebrating the Ordinary,' and it's rooted in the belief that we have to take delight in and acknowledge the ordinary every single day in order to work our way toward accomplishing the extraordinary.

Think about it. Life presents us with tens of thousands of days, each chock-full of opportunity. Yet, in the end, most people struggle to recall even twenty days that they would define as truly remarkable. Try it. Give yourself two minutes and write down in three or four words, the twenty most memorable days of your life off the top of your head. No scrolling back through Instagram for inspiration. Ready, set... go!

It's hard, isn't it? Don't worry, you're not alone. Most people can't even get to ten.

While those big days are no doubt impactful, we also must find time to rejoice on all the other days in between. In that lies the key to success. I'm no psychologist, but it's clear to me that people who are happy accomplish more than those who are not. My grandfather knew how important celebrating the ordinary was, and he wanted to do his part to ensure that I didn't end up like the others or, as he affectionally called them, "miserable sons of bitches."

I find my colleagues are often quick to buy into the concept of celebrating the ordinary, but they are sometimes challenged to implement this daily practice into their professional routine. Look, it's no secret that people tend to be creatures of habit, but those that revel in their daily success enjoy greater satisfaction, purpose, and meaning in their professional existence. Celebrating the ordinary creates small, attainable goals, which organically fuel forward momentum over the aimless toil that occurs when our eyes are set on some far-off objective that almost always seems insurmountable. How is that productive? Hint: it's not. If in the end, you can look back at literally hundreds of small, daily celebrated accomplishments, it will not only make the journey to achieving the extraordinary a lot more enjoyable, but also a lot more probable. Building a culture for a sales team based on these principals provides team members with a daily sense of both purpose and autonomy that is paramount, especially to Millennials (and don't forget the Gen Zs behind them) who now make up the largest part of our workforce.

So, if you take anything from my story, I hope it's that you will make a conscious effort to take a minute, maybe even two minutes, to celebrate the ordinary in your life. Every day. It may or may not make you more successful, but it will certainly make you happier and, if you think about it, success without happiness is actually worthless.

CHAPTER 18

LEADERSHIP AS EASY AS 1-2-3 AND A-B-C

By **TOM WIGGINS**

Four decades ago, as a college freshman in 1979, I began to understand the distinction between the most basic definition of a "professional" as someone who is paid to perform a service and the more nuanced definition of a "professional" as a person who has achieved mastery of their craft.

In the first example, someone working in the world's oldest profession is clearly "professional." In the second example, we think of people who are outstanding within their particular area of expertise in fields as diverse as business, sports, politics, academics, the arts, and the military, among others.

Working in an entry-level union job during high school, I made good money but didn't feel that the basic work that I did qualified me as a professional or a master of the craft. It was during my college internships that I began to have an appreciation for this higher level of professionalism. I apprenticed in a wide range of disciplines with an eye towards learning from the best... and sometimes learning what not to do from the rest.

As my professional development continued after college and graduate school, I came to appreciate the quality of leadership. Long a believer in the old adage that the harder you work, the luckier you get, I have been lucky enough to observe outstanding examples of leadership in a variety of professional settings.

The Accidental Leader

My first brush with leadership was as an accidental leader in my first year of college. It was a pivotal experience. I was a 17-year-old college freshman when I joined a large national fraternity, Sigma Phi Epsilon (SigEp). Shortly after joining, I was elected president of the chapter. This was a tremendous change for me as I literally had no prior leadership experience. Heck, I'd never even been a recess line leader in elementary school.

How I became president of an organization that I had just joined was a result of a fundamental change in the fraternity system at that specific college at that time. That was the first year that a national fraternity was created at a college with an established system of local fraternities. This meant that there was no existing leadership within this new chapter; someone would need to fill the role of leading this new organization.

The accidental nature of my first brush with leadership came when I found myself being "voluntold" by others that I should seek election for the top spot of the newly established fraternity chapter. I chose to say yes and that made all the difference as we set about to create the organizational structure for the newly developing chapter.

In that initial experience as an accidental leader, I formed the basis of my leadership philosophy of 1-2-3 and A-B-C. This philosophy would be stated and re-stated by other leaders in the fraternity, in the world of management consulting after college, and in my later journeys through professional worlds as disparate as wealth management and automotive research and development.

The 1-2-3 and A-B-C of Leadership

Simply stated, the 1-2-3 process is illustrated as follows:

1. **Put the client's interests first.**
2. **Put the firm's interests second.**
3. **Your own success will flow from the above.**

Within each of these three areas, I visualize A-B-C as the driving force:

Always
Be
Creating

The 1-2-3 and the A-B-C provide a mnemonic, a simple pattern of numbers and letters, that jogs our memory and helps keep what's important at the forefront of our thought processes.

My Examples of 1-2-3 and A-B-C

In that earliest college fraternity experience, the 1-2-3 and A-B-C broke down as follows. The #1 priority was the needs of the local SigEp chapter, the #2 priority was the national SigEp organization, and the #3 priority was meeting my needs as an individual SigEp member. In terms of A-B-C, that meant building up a brand new SigEp chapter at that first college and then continuing my SigEp experience with that fraternity at the second college I transferred to. At my third and final college, I joined with other transfer students who had been SigEps at their prior colleges and together we restarted a dormant SigEp chapter before I graduated.

When I worked in management consulting, first came the client's needs on the engagement, second came the organizational needs of the consulting firm, and then my development as a consultant naturally developed from these. Both firms that I worked for in the years between college and graduate school were among the largest national firms in their respective fields of expertise: hotel development and real estate development. It was during this period that I experienced A-B-C in the context of consulting engagements that often involved thinking creatively about new development projects that literally had no historical precedent.

After graduate school, as I transitioned into wealth management, I put my investment clients at the top tier of the priority pyramid and put the firm's goals in the next tier, with my own success flowing down from the first two tiers. I worked in the then new area of Socially Responsible Investing (SRI), helping clients incorporate their personal values into their financial decisions as I created investment portfolios for them. This initially took the form of A-B-C when creating SRI investment portfolios at a large Wall Street firm; later, I implemented these ABCs as a branch manager at a boutique firm specializing in SRI.

Most recently, I transformed what began as a fantasy career as a solo test driver for an engineering company into managing projects and other test drivers in Southern California, Northern California, and three states in New England. At the top level of this 1-2-3 were the needs of the automotive companies (my clients), followed by the needs of the engineering company (my employer), and finally followed by my own need to grow as a test team leader. An example of the A-B-C as a lead driver was to effectively bridge the engineering, technician, marketing, government, and public relations groups during the development of a new test driver team focused on testing hydrogen fuel cell vehicles and fueling stations.

Throughout all of these experiences, I've sought to continuously improve my skill set as a professional. This process of continuing to seek improvement is often referred to as kaizen in Japanese management philosophy. I seek to learn from the leaders above me and translate those lessons into my own leadership.

Applying 1-2-3 and A-B-C in Your Life

So, how do you apply my simple guidelines of 1-2-3 and A-B-C in your own life? The marvelous thing is that the simplicity of these two principles can apply to all aspects of your life--relationships, family, and work come to mind immediately.

Within your primary relationship, you can think of how you might apply these guidelines to how you interact with your partner (and they with you). For example, maybe your role in the relationship is to handle the finances and it is up to you to take the lead managing the balance between revenues and expenses. Prioritize your household's necessary spending as #1, your saving as #2, and your excess accrues to #3. If there is no excess, you'll need to take steps to increase your income and/or decrease your expenses. You develop your own ABCs and you decide what to "create" in areas like increasing net worth or charitable giving.

Expanding from your primary relationship, you might apply this to your family whether as a parent, stepparent, foster parent, pet parent, or any other role in which others look to your leadership within the family unit. Think of your child's needs first, then how those needs fit into the family, and then yourself. You are the one to Always Be Creating whatever your family needs to keep moving forward.

Finally, and most pertinent to the topic of business leadership, you can consider how 1-2-3 and A-B-C might apply within your profession in general and your organization specifically. Let's dive in to a few examples of how we might apply this.

Professional Examples of 1-2-3 and A-B-C

In sales, you consider your prospect's needs first and your sales group's needs second; then your personal sales goals will flow from those first two. Think to yourself, "How will I Always Be Creating the solution that best meets the needs of my client and my sales group, as well as fulfills my personal sales goals?"

In the political arena, your constituents are your #1 priority (or, at least, they should be), followed by the policies of your political party, and lastly by your own political ambitions. In modern politics, breach of this principle may be more apparent than adherence. Always Be Creating political solutions that best serve those you serve--the ones who elected you in the first place.

In academics, like in many other disciplines, the 1-2-3 may in fact be conditional... "It depends." As a teacher at the elementary or high school or undergraduate levels, your students are your top priority. In a doctoral or post-doctoral setting, research is of paramount importance and is therefore the first priority. The needs of your educational institution would come next and your academic success will then flow from your students' success or your research success. You will A-B-C the pathways that lead to academic discovery.

Sports are another case of "it depends," as the 1-2-3 process hinges on whether you are competing in individual disciplines or as part of a sports team. As a young ski racer, my #1 priority was to finish in the best possible position in each race of my chosen events, slalom and giant slalom. If I had taken the route of playing more traditional American team sports (like football, basketball, or baseball) my #1 priority would have been to make sure that my performance made the best possible contribution to winning each game. In either example, your individual performance serves the team and further develops your skills as an athlete. Participants in individual and team sports have a mindset to A-B-C the physical condition, the sport-specific skill sets, and the mental discipline needed to win.

Whither the artist? How can we apply 1-2-3 and A-B-C to something as seemingly ethereal and esoteric as art? Quite easily, in fact. Whether it's music or poetry or painting or any other aspect of the artistic world, it's the completion of the artistic piece first (which, in the case of commissioned art, is another example of Client First), then the development of a portfolio of work, and, if talent and luck and numerous other factors meet, perhaps the artist will acquire personal fame. Always Be Creating is a self-evident truth for the artist.

The military concept of Mission First is one that I frequently discussed with a Marine who was my right-hand guy on numerous recent projects. While the mission might be paramount, a close second is the needs of the military division and third is the needs of the individual who works in service of the mission and the division. Whether preparing for battle or strategizing for some other purpose, Always Be Creating a plan for the mission.

Being a member of the clergy can also fit within the framework of 1-2-3 and A-B-C. One could consider multiple approaches to this within faith-based work: #1 could be the needs of the people in the church, temple, or mosque pews or #1 could be the targeted needs of a specific part of the community for a faith-based nonprofit. Second might be the goals of the particular organization and rounding out the third spot might be the needs of the individual clergy member. In a faith-based environment, A-B-C can be taken to mean Always Be Creating a better world, rather than Attendance-Buildings-Cash that some religious institutions focus on.

Leadership, Condensed

As with all facets of our development, developing leadership skills is a lifetime process. We learn, we teach, we observe, we refine, and we repeat. We continually add to our skill sets within our professional roles, keeping in mind the 1-2-3 priorities (Client 1st-Firm 2nd-Self 3rd)and the driving force of A-B-C (Always Be Creating).

Cheers to your own success, focusing on 1-2-3 and A-B-C!

CONCLUSION

One of my all-time favorite speeches on how to win in business is called "Just Do It" by Art Williams (watch it on YouTube). It has served as a type of guidepost for me on my personal journey to developing into the type of leader I want to become.

Art says:

"If you want to win in business, you got to be a leader. Leadership is everything. You show me anything in these United States that wins, I'll show you a leader at work. You show me a successful church, boy scout troop, club, football team, or business and I'll show you something run by a leader."

I've watched that speech hundreds of times throughout the years. It was one of my favorites to blast in the office before starting my day for a long time. The interesting thing is that as I've matured in business, that speech has taken on new meaning and complexity. Maturity, age, and the benefit of hindsight tends to bless us with new lenses through which to see more clearly along the way when we are active participants in our own self-development.

It is my hope that this book will serve as its own type of guidepost for you now and in the future. I hope that you will be able to refer to it or any of the others in the Money Matters leadership series to gauge how you have progressed as a leader through your career.

To share your stories, connect with me on Instagram @AskAdamTorres

Wishing you much success,

Adam Torres

APPENDIX

Adam Torres | Introduction | Page iii
Co-Founder Money Matters Top Tips
MoneyMattersTopTips.com
Instagram: @AskAdamTorres
Twitter: @AskAdamTorres

Alexander Sonkin | Chapter 1 | Page 1
Founder, Virtual Family Office Hub (VFO Hub, LLC)
https://www.linkedin.com/in/alexsonkin/
www.vfohub.com, info@vfohub.com

Alexander Christian Swiger | Chapter 2 | Page 13
Entrepreneur
alexanderswiger@hotmail.com

Angy Chin | Chapter 3 | Page 21
Founder & President, BIC Group LLC
Founder & President, BIC App LLC
Co-Founder & Board Member, CA Solar Exchange dba Llumetec
angy@bicgroup.biz
linkedin.com/in/angychin

Arminda Figueroa | Chapter 4 | Page 33
Chief Marketing Connector & Founder
Latin2Latin Marketing + Communications
L2LMarketing.com

Gail Tolbert | Chapter 5 | Page 43
Founder & CEO of OutsideTheBox, LLC
www.think-outside-thebox.com
gailktolbert@gmail.com
Linked In: https://www.linkedin.com/in/gailtolbert/
Twitter: @tolbertg

Jeff A. Neumeister | Chapter 6 | Page 55
Owner and CEO of Neumeister & Associates, Inc.
jeff@neumeistercpa.com
LinkedIn: /ForensicAcct
Facebook: @neumeistercpa
Instagram: @neumeistercpa
Yelp: neumeister-and-associates-burbank

Jennifer DiMotta | Chapter 7 | Page 65
LinkedIn: https://www.linkedin.com/in/jenniferdimotta/

Kate Yoak | Chapter 8 | Page 63
CEO of Lean Street Company
https://leanstreet.io/
LinkedIn:https://www.linkedin.com/in/kateyoak/

Lauralie Levy | Chapter 9 | Page 85
CEO Crowd Siren
Social Media & Marketing
CrowdSiren.com
Twitters: @lauralielevy

Lisa Thomson, DC, CFMP, CME | Chapter 10 | Page 95
Founder of Back Body Mind Chiropractic
https://backbodymind.com/
Instagram: @DrLisaThomson

Marco Baldocchi | Chapter 11 | Page 103
CEO and President of Marco Baldocchi Group
CEO and Co-Founder Emotel Reality
CEO and Co-Founder On Web
mb@marcobaldocchi.com
LinkedIn: marcobaldocchi
Twitter: @marco_baldocchi
Facebook: @marco.baldocchi
Instagram: @marco.baldocchi
Marco Baldocchi Group inc. www.marcobaldocchi.com

Marguerita Cheng | Chapter 12 | Page 115
CEO at Blue Ocean Global Wealth
https://www.blueoceanglobalwealth.com/
Twitter @BlueOceanGW
LinkedIn: www.linkedin.com/in/margueritacheng

Parag Amin | Chapter 13 | Page 123
Principal at Law Office of Parag L. Amin, P.C.
https://www.lawpla.com
Parag@lawpla.com

Qamar Zaman | Chapter 14 | Page 131
Chief Awesomeness Officer at KISSPR.COM
QZ@KissPR.com
KissPR.com

Regina Newberry | Chapter 15 | Page 147
CEO of OutDo Wit Consulting Group, LLC
(Management Consulting)
Author of *Recognizing A Cash Cow~Honing In on Your Company's Best Asset-THE PEOPLE*
reginanewberry@outdowitconsulting.com
outdowitconsulting.com
recognizingacashcowbook.com
Linkedin: regina-newberry-ceo
Twitter: @outdowitconsult
Facebook: @recognizecashcowbook

Dr. Riadh Fakhoury | Chapter 16 | Page 157
Founder and CEO of Vestech Partners, LLC
https://www.vestechpartners.com/

Scott Von Deylen | Chapter 17 | Page 169
LinkedIn: scott-von-deylen

Thomas Wiggins | Chapter 18 | Page 179
tom@thomasvwiggins.com
linkedin.com/in/tomwiggins

The PODCAST MATTERS SCHOOL

Why Did I Start This School?

Every day I interview business owners, entrepreneurs and executives. I've done over 500 podcast episodes in the last year alone.

Depending on when you read this, I'll likely be over 1,000 episodes.

Many of the people I interview ask me to help them launch their own podcast. My ultimate goal is to help people spread their story and message. So of course I started helping people one by one. I figured, the more people I can help start podcasts, the more people I would help spread their message. Mission accomplished.

But then things got a little out of control. See, I like many have a habit of over committing. It got to the point to where helping people launch their own podcast was taking up more time than I had for the project.

So I was faced with two choices.

One, tell people "no" I don't have the time to help them.

Or, create a podcast school for those who want to launch a podcast or continue to grow their reach for an exiting podcast they already have.

Obviously, I wanted to continue helping people, so the school was born.

What Makes This School Different?

First, this course is NOT designed for people looking for a way to make a quick buck.

The community is designed for busy professionals who have always wanted to podcast but have never had the time or "know how" to get started. Another group who will benefit are the "part time" podcasters who can't quite figure out how to grow their audience.

While I'm not claiming that I've seen all podcast courses made, I can tell you that when I was just getting started it seemed like all of the courses were really long and felt like part time jobs to complete. Well I wasn't looking for a part time job, I had a business already, I just wanted to podcast.

So my commitment to you is that each lesson I bring will be straight to the point. Most videos will be under five minutes and many times will be two minutes or less. Why? Because you don't need to hear me drone on. You just need the information so you can act. Less time learning and more time in action is what will grow your podcast.

Finally, it's kinda weird for me to say this, considering I had almost 14 years of wealth management experience under my belt before going full time into media about 3 years ago, but - this is what I do for a living.

This is not a "side hustle" for me. I get paid to podcast, not just to teach. Why do I tell you this? Well, to be up front, you want to learn from someone who lives what they are teaching. You don't want someone experimenting with YOUR time.

For more information visit:
MoneyMattersTopTips.com/PodcastSchool

Happy Podcasting!

Adam Torres

The

MONEY MATTERS

BOOK CLUB

SAVE UP TO 50%!

How it works:

STEP #1:

Choose payment plan *(quarterly or yearly)*

STEP #2:

We mail you one new "Money Matters" book quarterly

(4 books yearly, currently U.S. only)

STEP #3:

Receive your new book on your doorstep and enjoy!

(No contracts, cancel anytime)

And thats it, simple, stress free and stable.

For more details visit: **MoneyMattersTopTips.com/bookclub**

OTHER AVAILABLE TITLES

In the original edition of Money Matters (Business Leaders Edition), Adam Torres features 15 top professionals who share their lessons on leadership. In these pages, through inspiring stories, you'll discover:

- How to create a clear path for growth.
- Why every business should act like a media company.
- How to build a community to last a lifetime.
- Lessons learned from professional soccer.
- How to maintain a well-connected brain for peak performance.
- How to create harmony through union in business.
- And much more.

Embracing diversity and inclusion in a rapidly changing business landscape can be challenging. Are you and your organization positioned properly for this new age of connectivity? Torres features fourteen top Asian leaders who share their lessons on diversity, equality and inclusion.

Navigating the world of real estate can be stressful. Are you getting closer or further from your goals? Finance guru Adam Torres is here to help you move forward. His guide, Money Matters, features 15 top professionals who share lessons from their more than 250 years of combined experience.

Purchase at **MoneyMattersTopTips.com/store**

In this clear, concise manual, financial expert Adam Torres goes over the basics of personal finance and investing and shows you how to grow your wealth. Torres makes sure you are prepared for whatever life throws your way. It's never too early to think about the future and his book will give you the right tools to tackle it.

Purchase at **MoneyMattersTopTips.com/store**

This workbook has been designed specifically for individuals like you who are dedicated to improving the results in all areas of your life. By following the ideas and exercises presented to you in this transformational workbook, you can move yourself into the realm of top achievers worldwide.

Download for free at **moneymatterstoptips.com/store.**

Made in the USA
Columbia, SC
03 November 2019

82592452R00124